W9-BWB-474

# WORD
# BIBLICAL
# THEMES

General Editor
# David A. Hubbard

Old Testament Editor
# John D. W. Watts

New Testament Editor
# Ralph P. Martin

# WORD
# BIBLICAL
# THEMES

## 1,2 Corinthians

### RALPH P. MARTIN

WORD PUBLISHING
Dallas · London · Sydney · Singapore

1, 2 CORINTHIANS
Word Biblical Themes

Scripture quotations in the Corinthian letters are from the author's own translation. Quotations identified as RSV are from the Revised Standard Version of the Bible, copyrighted 1946, 1952, 1971 by the Division of Christian Education of the National Council of Churches of Christ in the U.S.A. and are used by permission.

Unless otherwise indicated, all Scripture quotations are from the author's own translation.

**Library of Congress Cataloging-in-Publication Data**

Martin, Ralph P.
    1–2 Corinthians.

    (Word Biblical themes)
    Includes index.
    1. Bible.  N.T.  Corinthians—Theology.  I. Title.
II. Title: First–second Corinthians.  III. Series.
BS2675.2.M35   1988       227'.206       88-33821
ISBN 0-8499-0623-7

*Printed in the United States of America*
 9 8 0 1 2 3 9 RRD 9 8 7 6 5 4 3 2 1

For
Nathan Douglas Knode
born on February 15, 1987
true gift of God

# CONTENTS

# FOREWORD

Paul's letters to the Corinthian church have always held a special fascination for the people of Christ. In them we read of our foibles, temptations, joys, and possibilities. And through them we see at work the patience, strength, courage, and wisdom of the great apostle.

It does not stretch the imagination unduly to see our times as a neo-Corinthian age. We too have to grapple with factions quarreling over which leader is best; we too are forced to deal with sexual immorality in the believing community; we too have to cope with controversy in the use and importance of spiritual gifts. Ralph Martin's insightful, informed, and winsome treatment of these important letters is an outstanding contribution to all who care about biblical truth and seek to live by it.

*Word Biblical Themes*, a companion series to the *Word Biblical Commentary*, seeks to distill the theological essence of the biblical books as interpreted in the more technical series and to serve it up in ways that will enrich the preaching, teaching, worship, and discipleship of God's people. Dr.

Martin, as New Testament Editor of both series, is admirably qualified to contribute an early volume to the *Themes*. His works on *2 Corinthians* and *James* in WBC have set high standards and have already been warmly acclaimed by scholars and pastors alike.

This exposition of the teachings and settings of the Epistles to Corinth is sent forth in the hope that it will contribute to the vitality of God's people, renewed by the Word and the Spirit and ever in need of renewal.

Fuller Theological Seminary
Pasadena, California

David A. Hubbard
General Editor
*Word Biblical Themes*
*Word Biblical Commentary*

The two letters of Paul to the church at Corinth still cast a spell on the modern reader who is prepared to enter with some imagination and thought into the scene they describe. The one outstanding feature of that scene is the vitality and exuberance of these Christians in the busy metropolitan center of Corinth. Paul had a special place in his affection for these people. The fact that he did not abandon them when they proved so obstinate says much about Paul's role as a caring pastor and leader.

But the lessons to be drawn from these letters are much more than those of pastoral management and personal relationships, important as these surely are. At the heart of the Corinthian debate is the meaning of the gospel and the role of the church as a worshiping and witnessing community. These three words may well be placed on the agenda of the church today: gospel, worship, witness. They sum up what is the church's real business in the world of our day. The *gospel* defines our message; *worship* is the church's reason for existing; and *witness* is the face we show to the world in all its plight. While there may be other pressing items to be debated and implemented from time to time, these, I am persuaded, are the continuing agenda items for the church in every age and setting. Any study of 1 and 2 Corinthians is bound to be important as we wrestle with the way Paul dealt with these issues, and how he speaks the Word of God to our concerns today.

It has proven a daunting task to compose a short and (we hope) readable account of Biblical Themes on 1 and 2 Corinthians. Yet the effort in prospect seemed worthwhile, if challenging; and as I look back on it, it has been a rich experience. Whether it has succeeded is not for the author to say.

These letters offer a valuable case study of life in an early Christian community. They have been examined from a variety of angles, with the current interest in sociology finding here a well-stocked seam of data waiting to be mined. Books by Baird, Judge, Meeks, and Theissen will come to mind.[1] Another recent interest has focused on Paul's literary and rhetorical styles in debate with the Corinthians, with some valuable studies by Murphy-O'Connor, P. Marshall, and Talbert contributing much to our understanding.[2] I gratefully pay tribute to what one can learn from these approaches, though it is clear that in a little book like this, much must go unmentioned, if not unnoticed.

I have tried to concentrate on and bring out the main items in the Corinthian discussion, and have chosen to highlight a few central theological concerns as providing a gateway to the meaning of the letters. Obviously in consequence many themes have been passed over, and I regret this. Further help to the would-be reader is provided by two sources I will suggest. Shortly to appear will be a full-scale exposition on 1 Corinthians written by James A. Davis, of Trinity Episcopal School for Ministry, in Ambridge, Pennsylvania, in the *Word Biblical Commentary* series, which will offer a comprehensive treatment of all the problem passages ignored here. Mention may be made of the present writer's *2 Corinthians*, also in the WBC series, and his earlier (1984) title, *The Spirit and the*

*Congregation: Studies in 1 Corinthians 12–15.* I have tried not to duplicate material from these larger books.

If one ruling theme pervades both letters it is the meaning of apostleship or, as we may say, Christian leadership. The Corinthian books were written with leaders, both clergy and lay, in mind, and so it is pertinent to hear again what one of our best commentators has to say on this subject:

> "Apostle" [as] a powerful and imposing person, standing out for all the rights he could possibly claim, performing miracles, and accepting adulation and support of those whom he was able to impress . . . that [such] represent a permanent threat to Christianity is written on every page of church history and is in itself a sufficient reason for the continued study of 2 Corinthians.

This well-spoken analysis and tribute is even more timely today than in 1973 when C. K. Barrett wrote the words.[3] May this little handbook assist also in directing our attention to the role of the congregation and its leaders in the modern church.

I am grateful for the secretarial help of Shelley Theisen, and of Sandy Bennett with her team in the Word Processing Department at Fuller Theological Seminary, in preparing the manuscript.

*Ralph P. Martin*
*The University of Sheffield*
*Department of Biblical Studies*

# 1  PAUL'S FRIENDS AT CORINTH

The apostle Paul's first acquaintance with the city of Corinth came in A.D. 50 in the course of his second missionary journey. The record of his coming to Corinth is given in the narrative of Acts 18:1–20, where he appears in various roles. (a) As a tentmaker he associated with a Christian couple Aquila and his wife Priscilla (18:2, 3). This husband-and-wife team played a significant part in early Christianity as we see from Acts 18:24–26, Rom 16:3, and 1 Cor 16:19 where we learn of a Christian group that met in their home. (b) As a disputant Paul engaged in debate in the Jewish synagogue (Acts 18:4). In the excavation of the Corinth of Roman times a marble cornice block that could possibly have stood as the lintel of a synagogue doorway has been unearthed. It is inscribed with now broken wording, restored as "synagogue of the Hebrews." While the dating of this inscription is probably later than Paul's day, the presence of a strong Jewish element in the population is attested by the account in Acts 18. In particular, Crispus, a leader of the synagogue, is mentioned as a convert won over by Paul's preaching (Acts 18:8;

1 Cor 1:14). Another official of the Jewish meeting place, Sosthenes, is referred to both in the story of Acts 18:16 and in 1 Cor 1:1.

(c) In his ministry as a herald of the good news Paul had some success. According to Acts 18:5, with the arrival of his colleagues Silas and Timothy from Macedonia which evidently sent gifts for his Christian work, Paul was able to devote his time and energy exclusively to mission work. As a consequence he met with active opposition from within the Jewish community and had to remove to a new base of operations. This he found in the house of Titius Justus, a Gentile adherent. We may suppose that this move widened the appeal of his message. Many others were attracted to the gospel, several bearing Greco-Roman names. Gaius is mentioned as a convert Paul baptized (1 Cor 1:14). The family of Stephanas may be added to the list, according to 1 Cor 1:16. This man evidently became a leader of the infant congregation, since he is commended as one devoted with his family to Christian service (1 Cor 16:15), and he formed part of the later delegation that brought questions to the apostle in Ephesus (1 Cor 16:17). Fortunatus and Achaicus were the other two members whom the Corinthians deputed to visit Paul at the same time. A woman, Chloe (1 Cor 1:11), is spoken of in connection with her "family," a term meaning either her kinfolk or more likely her dependent workers. Phoebe, too, should be included in this short list. She is named as "deaconess" of the church at Cenchreae (Rom 16:1), the port of Corinth on its eastern side. The city stood on a narrow neck of land connecting two seas, and its geographical location played an important part in deciding its economic and political fortunes, as we shall see.

(d) The little cameo of Acts 18:9–11 reveals Paul as a truly human being in need of encouragement and cheer. The mission at Corinth was not easy, and there was much to discourage and disappoint God's servant. Luke's account of the oracle that came from the heavenly Lord mentions the promise of deliverance from physical danger ("no one shall set upon you to do you harm," v 10). The assurance is given that the Lord has "many people in this city," a pledge that turned out to be true in the sense that as a result of Paul's initial evangelism a congregation, meeting in various house groups, was established. We are able to identify by name no fewer than sixteen persons who became charter members of the infant Christian community.

The composition of the Corinthian church has been much discussed in recent years. A. Deissmann took the view, mainly on the basis of 1 Cor 1:26–29, that the majority of the members belonged to the poorer sections of the city's life.[1] In reply to this point of view it should be remarked that when Paul writes that "not many" were wise, powerful or of noble birth he does not imply "not any." E. A. Judge has come to an opposite conclusion, therefore.[2] He argues that Corinthian Christians, like many of Paul's converts, were part of the upper middle-class society. The fullest discussion is that provided by G. Theissen who has investigated the social stratification of the Christian community.[3] He gives due attention both to the evidence of 1 Cor 1:26–29 and 11:18 which speaks of "divisions," partly socioeconomic, that enabled the rich people to come early to the common meal but prevented the slave classes from arriving on time when all the food was set out (see 11:21, 33, 34), and also the counterbalancing data. In the latter category we may draw attention to the following:

Crispus is called the synagogue ruler, a title implying that he was responsible for the maintenance of the building and its necessary repairs. He could only have done this if he was a man of some wealth. The houses owned—or at least occupied—by Crispus and Stephanas (1 Cor 1:14; 16:15) along with Titius Justus, according to Acts 18:7, also testify to some social standing in the community. "Chloe's people" is another indirect witness to a woman of considerable social status. (iii) The clearest evidence is offered in the reference to Erastus who, in Rom 16:23, is described as "the city treasurer." Given the fact that Paul wrote this tribute and commendation of Erastus while he was at Corinth, and that in 1929 an inscription, dated to the second half of the first century, came to light, the likelihood that Erastus was both a prominent civic dignitary in Corinth and a member of the congregation there is strong.

Near the theater at Corinth the following fragmentary inscription can be seen. It runs:

[. . . ] ERASTVS PRO AEDILIT[AT]E S P STRAVIT

"Erastus in recognition of his aedileship laid [the pavement] at his own expense."

The name in question is not a common one, though it does appear in Acts 19:22 and 2 Tim 4:20 in connection with Paul's friends and in association with Corinth. The aedile was more like the modern director of public works, while the strict title for a finance officer in Greco-Roman cities is quaestor. But the two offices overlapped, and it is very likely that if Erastus is one and the same person in all these texts he was a person of some civic and social importance. So there are several strands of evidence to be brought together in assessing the social position of the Corinthians to whom Paul wrote.

(e) The final section of Acts 18:12–17 reveals Paul's own standing as a Roman. After a relatively long period of ministry he was set upon by the Jewish population and hauled before Gallio, the Roman proconsul of Achaia, the district of southern Greece whose affairs were administered from Corinth.

Since 27 B.C. Achaia had been placed under the jurisdiction of the Roman senate.[4] The background to this decision is found in Corinth's economic importance and geographical location. It had developed into a strong economic and urban center from the sixth century B.C. with an impressively large population. Its site on the isthmus which joined the Gulf of Corinth to the north and the Saronic Gulf to the east gave it an assured place as a commercial center, situated on the land and trade route from northern Greece to the Peloponnese and possessing two harbors.

In the war between the Achaean League of city-states and imperial Rome it opposed the ally of Rome, Sparta; and in turn Corinth was invaded and utterly destroyed by the Romans in 146 B.C. The city was deserted for about a century. In 44 B.C. Julius Caesar repopulated it, and dignified it with his own name as a Roman outpost. Its occupation as a Roman colony brought many settlers, and in turn led to the reestablishment of Corinth as a city of fine buildings, shops, theaters, and houses, with Roman influence to be seen everywhere. The interlude in Acts 18:12–17 with Paul the Roman citizen brought in front of the bema or raised platform of Lucius Junius Gallio, older brother of the philosopher Seneca in A.D. 51 is quite in character with all that is known from ancient history and modern archaeology of Roman Corinth.

Corinth's roads were laid out in the Roman pattern, with the bema in the civic center modeled on the rostra of the Roman forum. In Paul's day the city teemed with life. Building projects begun under the emperors Tiberius and Claudius were underway—a fact which Paul may well have exploited in his writing (1 Cor 3:10, 11). The city was vibrant with prosperity, and proud of its reputation as the pleasure palace of the ancient world. Its trade, said the geographer Strabo, brought much wealth, and the banks flourished, according to Plutarch. Artisans employed their skills with bronze artifacts, pottery manufacture, and especially Corinthian lamps made of terra cota which were well-known throughout the ancient world (cf. 2 Cor 4:7). Agriculture also was a key to Corinth's prosperity, and Paul can use the imagery of the field and the farm to make a point to his urban readers (1 Cor 3:6-9; 9:7, 10; 2 Cor 9:6-10).

The religious life of Corinth is well-attested. An impressive Doric temple still stands in ruins on a small promontory overlooking the site. Since Corinth's inception as a city it had sponsored the Isthmian Games among the Greek states, held in celebration of the sea god Poseidon, and it is conceivable that the biannual event coincided with Paul's visit in A.D. 50-51. If so, some of his language and idioms may well be accounted for (for example, 1 Cor 9:24-27). The fountain of Peirene, though best preserved of the Corinthian fountains, is later than Paul's day.

On the west side of the forum is an ornamental fountain in honor of Poseidon and Aphrodite, the Greek goddess of life, beauty, and passion, whom the Romans called Venus. Her main temple was set on Acrocorinth, a mountain fifteen hundred feet in elevation that dominates the site. Strabo's remark that a thousand prostitutes serviced this temple now is treated with extreme caution, and the moral climate of Corinth, often regarded as the epitome of immoral ways, seems to have been no worse than other Greek cosmopolitan cities. The way the Corinthians gave to the Greek lexicon a new word, "to Corinthianize," meaning to indulge one's appetites to the full, is also to be taken with reserve. There were political reasons why writers wished to denigrate Corinth. On the other side, however, we may remember that Rom 1:18-32 with its grim exposé of life in Greco-Roman society was a passage written at Corinth. And it is undeniable that Paul encountered a wide variety of moral problems in his subsequent pastoral dealings with his Corinthian converts.

In summary, into this city Paul brought the message of Christ. A church was formed, and it grew. Paul's friends, whom he regarded as his children (1 Cor 4:15; 2 Cor 6:13), were a mixed lot, a veritable cross-section of society in this cosmopolitan city of southern Greece, famed for its pretensions to wisdom, its popular culture, its trade, its harbors, and its love of life. By the grace of God and the ministry of his servant a church was established. For reasons that we may piece together from Paul's wider dealings with the mother church and its leaders at Jerusalem, with Antioch and Ephesus, Corinth became of pivotal concern to Paul at this stage in his missionary career. Much to do with Paul's relations with Corinth is still unclear. But one fact stands out. Of all the congregations founded by his apostolic service none posed so many problems as the Corinthians, and no group of Christians so well illustrates what was to Paul the cost in pastoral care and concern of being a servant of Christ to his people. The remark Paul makes, at the climax of his tribulation list in 2 Cor 11:23-28, must surely have reflected his recent experience in his dealings with those who first read these words, "Aside from all the other things, there is the daily pressure that concern for all the congregations brings me" (11:28). No congregation brought Paul more "concern" (lit. anxiety) than the church at Corinth.

We now turn to consider why this was so.

### Factions and frictions at Corinth

By various routes Paul learned that all was not well with the infant community. But to understand the issues we must first try to fit together Paul's relations with Corinth once he left the city. After more than a year and a half of living and teaching among them the apostle moved on (Acts 18:11, 18). He came eventually to Ephesus as his next major base of operations (Acts 18:21; 19:1), where he settled for an extended period of two years (Acts 19:10). Luke's narrative passes over much that transpired in that period. From the data provided in the letters Paul wrote to Corinth during

*Paul's Friends at Corinth*

this time (say, A.D. 52–54) we can put together a probable itinerary of his movements and contacts.

(a) Sometime after reaching Ephesus Paul wrote a letter to which he later refers in 1 Cor 5:9. This is now no longer extant, though some scholars believe that 2 Cor 6:14–7:1 may be a fragment of it on the ground that there is apparently a common theme. This has to do with the need to be separate from moral evil. But this identification is by no means compelling, as we shall see.

(b) Rumors and reports from Chloe's household (1 Cor 1:11) brought the news that the church at Corinth was split into groups. There was evidently a crisis of authority within the church. It centered on the question of leadership, and from 1 Cor 16:15–18 we may infer that the delegation that came from Corinth to Ephesus supported Paul's apostleship and understanding of the gospel. Other leaders, mentioned in 1 Cor 11:18, 19, appeared to have expressed a preference for apostles such as Peter or preachers such as Apollos (1 Cor 1:12; 3:22).

(c) About the same time presumably Paul received a letter from the Corinthians asking for his advice and guidance on certain issues affecting marital problems, the ordering of worship, and relations with the outside world (1 Cor 7:1; 8:1). There was some uncertainty about the nature of spiritual gifts (12:1) with which the Corinthians were richly endowed (1:7).

(d) Paul met the situation created by these matters as he wrote the letter known as 1 Corinthians. It was taken to Corinth perhaps by Timothy whose mission is commended in 1 Cor 4:17 (see RSV, marg. "I am sending to you Timothy . . . to remind you of my ways in Christ").

(e) About this time a more serious crisis broke out with the centerpoint the authority of Paul himself. Perhaps Timothy brought the news of it back to Ephesus, though Paul may not have been unprepared for it since he expresses himself forcefully in 1 Cor 4:18–21 and threatens that he will have to come himself to deal with some fomenting trouble.

At all events he did make a visit to deal with the issue in person. He later alludes to this as a "painful visit" (2 Cor 2:1) because he was humiliated before the church, insulted by one prominent Corinthian believer, and forced to return to Ephesus in great distress. Two passages bear on his state of mind at that time: 2 Cor 2:1–11 and 7:8–13 as they indicate the steps he took to redress the wrong he felt he had suffered.

(f) He wrote a "tearful letter," at great cost to himself, to deal with the crisis (2 Cor 2:4; 7:8). This was carried to Corinth by Titus who was instructed to meet Paul on his return at Troas to where Paul now headed (2 Cor 2:12). In the interim, however, he was personally attacked in Ephesus and had to endure some form of physical assault (2 Cor 1:8–11) which may or may not be linked with the trial he speaks of as "fighting with beasts at Ephesus" (1 Cor 15:32). His life was seriously threatened and he was at the point of death—an extremity which is mirrored in much of the writing of 2 Cor chs 1–7. He was rescued by some divine interposition when all hope was gone, and lived to tell the tale of God's deliverance (see 2 Cor 4:8–15; 6:4–10).

(g) According to the plan outlined in 1 Cor 16:5–9 but subsequently modified by the need to visit Corinth in response to the critical situation referred to above, Paul left Ephesus to make his way to Macedonia. He came first to Troas where he hoped to meet Titus, but did not (2 Cor 2:13). Instead, therefore, of settling for a while at Troas he hurried over to Macedonia where, in fact, Titus was on his way to join him (2 Cor 2:13; 7:5–7). These must have been dark days for Paul. Not only had he suffered an attack from the outside, called "strife from without"; he also was faced with "fears from within," referred to in 2 Cor 7:5. We may identify the strife with the conflict endured at Ephesus, presumably with the Roman or Jewish authorities; and the fears were real fears engendered by the sad prospect that his investment in the lives of the Corinthians had gone for nothing. He had hoped to hear good news from Titus, who was not to be found at Troas.

(h) The sequel as Paul retells it was different. Titus came to Macedonia with a good report. The "letter of tears" had worked effectively. The rebellious leader was disciplined, and the Corinthian church had come back to Paul's side with renewed confidence. Such, evidently, was Titus' first reading of the situation, which lifted Paul's spirits and inspired him with fresh hope to believe that all was well. In that assurance he wrote 2 Cor 1-9, exulting in the triumph of his gospel (2:14) in spite of his own frailty (4:7) and insecurity, and explaining why his travel plans were revised (2 Cor 1:15-22). Above all, he expounded the message of reconciliation that had so recently been illustrated in the restoring of amicable relations between the church and the apostle. With the air cleared of suspicion it was time to charge Titus to return to Corinth to gather the collection for Jerusalem, which had been in abeyance (ch 8, 9).

(i) The last four chapters of 2 Cor are a puzzle. The view taken in this work is that they were written later than the composing of chs 1-9 and in the light of a new situation that threatened. According to 11:4, 12-15, emissaries arrived at Corinth, perhaps wishing to exploit the recent disaffection with Paul on the part of a section of the Corinthian leadership. These messengers were warmly received—but quickly reopened old wounds and insinuated that Paul was no true apostle or even not a Christian at all (10:7). He lacked all the qualities, gifts, and graces of an impressive apostolic figure; he was weak, insecure, and exposed to suffering at every turn.

When Paul sensed that new danger he wrote a blistering note, full of irony, invective, ridicule, and self-defense. This is 2 Cor 10-13, at the heart of which is Paul's "Fool's

Narrative" (11:16–12:10). It was dispatched to Corinth in a bold attempt to ward off present danger, and to accomplish what previous efforts had failed to achieve. Whether it succeeded or not, we cannot say for certain. Paul, according to Acts 20:2, came to Greece, presumably Corinth; and thence he sailed for Jerusalem with the collection, presumably including the money raised at Corinth. So we may believe that Paul's last letter was the most effective of all, and that the Corinthians were finally won over to his side.

But perhaps not finally in another sense. By the time of the letter called 1 Clement, written in A.D. 96 from Rome to Corinth, the church there was still racked by dissensions and infighting. The lesson is clear: there is no lasting reconciliation between antagonistic groups, even Christian groups, in this old eon, but every generation of believers needs to heed the apostle's call to live in peace and unity (2 Cor 13:11). And we can only respond by a continued reliance on those forces that moved and motivated Paul in his role as a reconciling agent to bring together alienated parties at Corinth: "the grace of the Lord Jesus Christ and the love of God and the fellowship of the Holy Spirit" (2 Cor 13:14).

The stage has been set to ask once more, what went wrong at Corinth? Why were there "factions" and "frictions"? And what were the real issues underlying the surfacing of ugly situations and problems. Let us attempt an overview, with the details to be filled in as our later chapters unfold.

Here was a company of Christian people recently won over from pagan and pernicious ways (1 Cor 6:9–11; 12:2) and always in danger of relapsing into past habits and vices (2 Cor 12:20, 21). The threat to return to the corporate and personal life they had renounced and broken with by baptism into Christ was ever present and always real. More than once Paul had to warn them against a false security (e.g., 1 Cor 10:12) and a supposed immunity from moral dangers present in the society around them (e.g., 2 Cor 6:14–7:1).

*Paul's Friends at Corinth*

But more was at stake than just the menacing world which created an ambience of temptation and seduction. Temptation and seduction were real dangers (2 Cor 11:2, 3), but the ease with which some of the Corinthians fell suggests that powerful factors of another kind were at work to lead them astray. There were four.

(a) Divisions within the congregation, which seems to have been dispersed into several house groups, were a source of trouble. For one thing, it gave the impression that the church was split into factions each owning allegiance to Christian leaders (1 Cor 1:11-17). The root idea was taken from the practice common in the hellenistic mystery religions that the person who did the initiating, called a mystagogue, held some sort of special power over the initiates. He was their mentor and guide, and they were beholden to him. The Corinthians imagined that the same idea applied to the service of baptism. To have been baptized by Paul was a great privilege for some. They then looked down on others who had not had that privilege (see 1 Cor 12:15-26 for this kind of superior attitude). Other believers were proud of their allegiance to Peter (called Cephas, his Jewish name) who had come to Corinth after Paul's first visit (1 Cor 9:5). Paul includes Cephas in the recital of the resurrection appearances (1 Cor 15:5) but he is quick to add that both he and Peter shared a common faith (15:11).

Apollos too was greatly admired by some, perhaps chiefly on the score that he was an eloquent preacher (Acts 18:24) and had greatly assisted believers in Achaia (Acts 18:27) who valued his special emphasis on argument and debate in refuting the Jewish objectors. Paul, by contrast, seemed to be an unlearned preacher with no rhetorical flair or gift of eloquence. He paled into insignificance when set alongside the powerful presence of Apollos with his recourse to wisdom to explain the mystery of God's salvation plan.

Yet Paul's determination not to use rhetorical devices to persuade his readers—at least at the time of writing 1 Cor and in reference to his first visit to the city—was intentional. He explains his reasoning in 1 Cor 2:1-5:

> When I came to you I came with no superiority in speech or wisdom, proclaiming to you the testimony of God. I decided to know nothing when among you but Jesus Christ, and even him as the crucified! I was with you in weakness and fear and much trembling; and my speech and proclamation were not in persuasive words of wisdom but were validated by the Spirit and by power, that your faith might depend not on human wisdom but on divine power.

The third name is less easy to pinpoint. Evidently there was a cry heard in the assembly that some belonged to Christ (1 Cor 1:12). If they formed a Christ-party, they may well have been extremely Jewish in their orientation and sought to revive a faith in Jesus as Israel's messiah and savior. Perhaps they were messianists who despised both Paul's claim to be apostle to the Gentiles and Apollos's wisdom which in turn had links with Alexandrian Judaism in Egypt, from where Apollos originated. These people would be wanting to press back to the simple Jesus of the earthly ministry and to be linked with him in a way Paul mentions (and discredits) in 2 Cor 5:16 by calling it "knowing Christ after the flesh," as an earthly messiah. Or else, if this party is seen in the reference in 2 Cor 10:7 it became a badge of distinction to have seen Jesus in his earthly life. Since Paul did not qualify on that point, he was dismissed as inferior. But there is no certainty here.

Several facts make it improbable that there ever was a Christ-party in rivalry to these apostolic groups mentioned.

In 1 Cor 3:21 the human names alone are given, with no mention of a Christ group. Similarly, in 1 Clement 47:3, only the names of Paul, Cephas, and Apollos are given as the way in which the Corinthians formed partisan groups. Thirdly, using 2 Cor 10:7 for another reason, we may argue that belonging to Christ was Paul's own claim. This leads to the conclusion that 1:12 should be read as climaxing in Paul's own retort by way of denouncing all parties:

Each of you says, "I belong to Paul"; "I to Apollos"; "I to Cephas." But I belong to Christ.

The last remark, then, is Paul's own confession, akin to what he says of himself in 1 Cor 11:1.

Charles Wesley's stanza is exactly Paul's point:

Names, and sects, and parties fall;
Thou, O Christ, art all in all.

Paul sternly sets his face against all such divisions which so disfigured the Corinthian assembly. Baptism is a rite of initiation into one body (1 Cor 12:12, 13, 25), and is administered in the name of Christ, not an apostolic figure, however revered. His own task is not to gather disciples but to proclaim the gospel (1 Cor 1:17), which is his distinctive calling in life (1 Cor 9:16; 2 Cor 4:6). In any case, men and women come to faith not through human agency but as the gift of the Spirit (1 Cor 12:3). What then is Apollos? what is Paul? are his questions to his childish readers (3:1-9); not "who" but "what" is the issue. Both persons are accredited leaders and worthy of honor; but both are equally "servants through whom you came to believe" (3:5).

This conclusion is reached at 4:6 and 7 which stands at the close of the section (3:5-4:7) within the Letter Body (identified by Dahl[5] as 1:10-4:21). Paul has written about Apollos and himself so that the Corinthians may learn by this illustration—as a child copies handwriting in ancient schooling, making the letters neither too large nor too small—not to exceed the limits laid down. Those limits are seen as the Lord of the church assigns ministry to each one (3:5), and so the Corinthians are not to behave arrogantly by favoring one preacher against the other (4:6). So let no one boast about men (3:21), since all men and women in God's service can only fulfill their calling as they promote Christ (a theme to which Paul returns in 2 Cor 10:15–18).

(b) The Corinthians had but a precarious hold on Christian morality. The evidence for this shows itself in several problems that came to the surface both in their inquiries of Paul and his replies. There was evident pride in immoral conduct of the worst kind (1 Cor 5:1–13); a breakdown of the community life (6:1–8), especially at the common meal table (11:17–22); and a division over the issue of how far one's conscience may stretch when it comes to attending feasts with idol-worshipers (8:1–13; 10:14–33). More seriously still, sexual mores at Corinth were lax to the point of condoning prostitution (6:12–20) and associating with people of bad disposition without regard to the baneful effects of such friendships (1 Cor 15:33; 2 Cor 6:14–7:1).

Paul's response lies in sounding a clarion call to the highest ethical standards, based on applying one's redemption to a life of dedication to a holy Lord (1 Cor 5:7, 8); an assertion of the *koinonia* that unites believers as one body in one Spirit under one Lord; and a concern for the Christian neighbor whose "upbuilding" (*oikodome* is Paul's favorite word in these chapters, to be observed shortly) is always to be sought by Christians (1 Cor 10:33; 14:5, 12, 26) and the primacy of love (*agape*) whose traits are evident in the one chapter Paul devotes to its praise and practice (1 Cor 13).

(c) In a church replete with gifts of the Holy Spirit (1 Cor 1:7) there was utter confusion about which "gifts-in-grace" (*charismata*) were to be sought and prized (1 Cor 14:12; see 12:31 which reads as if it gave the point of view of the Corinthians). The special manifestation of ecstatic speech, called "speaking in tongues" or "tongues of angels" (13:1), and women's ministries in prophetic oracles were evidently highly regarded (1 Cor 12:29, 30; 14:4-19, 22-25, 33b-38). But while Paul was prepared to give some sanction to both Corinthian worship practices he was aware that both glosso-lalic speech and women's prophetic ministries were fraught with dangerous consequences when they were allowed to get out of hand and promote a wrongheaded understanding of corporate worship.

His concern then is to establish priorities in the interest of two sides to public worship that most effectively set forth the gospel. They are, first, the need for control and restraint since God does not sanction disorder or unseemly behavior (1 Cor 14:33, 40), and, then, a desire to promote those parts of worship which will lead the outsider or interested in-quirer to be impressed with the presence of God (1 Cor 14:23-25) and to be able to enter intelligently into the mean-ing of what the worship of God entails (1 Cor 14:16).

True worship catches up the human spirit into the pres-ence of the divine; but it equally has a rational, intelligible side that informs and quickens the mind (1 Cor 14:15). Those on the fringe of church life are more likely to be lastingly influenced if they are able to make sense of what Christian worship is designed to do; they will then not dis-miss the assembling of believers as a meeting place of those possessed by a demonic spirit (1 Cor 14:9, 23). A very great danger arises when professed Christians are uncontrollably led into blasphemous utterances (1 Cor 12:1-3).

(d) Most serious of all, as Paul judged the Corinthian scene, was a *theological error*. The importance of being able to pin-point what this wrongheaded notion was will be clear once we note that it explains most, if not all, of the symptoms that marred church life at Corinth. The root idea was that at baptism believers entered the kingdom of God in its fullness (1 Cor 4:8), and this belief inevitably led to the conclusion that there was no hope of a future resurrection (1 Cor 15:12). Not that the future resurrection was denied; rather, it was passed over as unnecessary since its reality had been telescoped into present experience. That, we may say, was the chief element in a type of theologizing that came to take hold at Corinth after Paul's departure from the city. But what caused its emergence?

The best guess we may make points to the hellenistic ideas of "spirit" (*pneuma*). In a Greco-Roman city like Corinth it is a reasonable assumption that religious life would be dominated by the power of "spirit," a divine force that came irresistibly on those who opened their lives to its influence and carried them away, often into a trance-like state and often into erratic and bizarre behavior. There is concrete evidence for this in 1 Cor 12:2:

> You know that, when you were pagans, you were led away to dumb idols, as you were continually led.

Paul, in 1 Cor 6:9-11, harks back to the old way of life from which his readers had been set free. But it is clear that with his warning, "Don't be deceived," the pull of the old life was still being felt. The Corinthians were in constant danger of being drawn back—not only to immoral ways (which was bad enough) but to pagan thought patterns which, they imagined, could be accommodated to their profession as Christians. Much of Paul's Corinthian correspondence is taken up with seeking to unmask this false step and to raise strong theological objections to the error that was at the heart of Corinthian beliefs and practices.

"Spirit" was for them a key term, as we learn from 1 Cor 14:12 when read in the light of 14:1:

> Since you are eager in striving for "spirits," seek to excel
> for the building up of the church.

They traced the incoming of "spirit"—now linked with the Holy Spirit—into their lives and experience to what occurred in baptism, perhaps appealing to Paul's teaching about being raised with Christ to newness of life (cf. Rom 6:1-14; Col 3:1). They misunderstood this teaching, however, at one significant point. Thinking of themselves as risen with Christ they imagined they already had entered upon an angelic existence. Three parts of Corinthian church life and worship are now explained, as our later chapter will show. (i) Their marriage customs involved a type of spiritual union in which normal married relations were despised as "fleshly" since true believers, like the angels, were sexless (1 Cor 7:1-7, 36-40); (ii) "tongues of angels" (1 Cor 13:1) were a sign of the new age already begun and meant to be enjoyed in its present power; (iii) female members in exercising prophetic gifts of speech were breaking free from the mutual constraints of marriage, and as a badge of their full emancipation were discarding a head covering (1 Cor 11:2-16) and were laying claim to being innovative teachers (1 Cor 14:31-40). But the reason for their bid for independence was not sociological or feminist; rather, it rested on their supposed baptismal status as "like the angels of God" for whom there is no marriage or sexual distinction (see Luke 20:35, 36).

The Corinthian watchword was, therefore, "freedom" (1 Cor 6:12; 10:23), which was taken to an extreme, notably in the areas of sexual promiscuity and license. At the heart of a wrong religious idea was the practical misstep that led either to asceticism (as in 1 Cor 7) or indulgence without restraints (in 1 Cor 6). This puzzling situation can only be accounted for on one assumption. The Corinthians' false sacramentalism and narrow individualism led them to practices Paul can only view with great alarm. He offered in rebuttal two statements which recur throughout this correspondence. We mention them here in outline in the hope that they will bring us to the very center of Paul's theology in these letters.

*First,* he announced that he came to Corinth with the preaching of the cross as the main plank in his platform (1 Cor 1:18–2:5). We may stop to inquire why Paul found it needful to emphasize the centrality and cruciality of the cross to a Christian congregation. The answer is that the Corinthians were in danger of allowing the cross to be swallowed up in the glory of the resurrection. The resurrection for them was the kingpin of their baptismal experience and it brought the gift of "spirit" and the new age in its full power. The cross, then, was but a station on the road to Christ's glory in which they shared here and now. For Paul this understanding is fatally flawed. The cross is a historical event, since "Christ died for our sins" (1 Cor 15:3; 2 Cor 5:14–21), but equally it sets the pattern for all Christian living. It issues a call of dying to live, reminding those who profess the faith of Christ crucified that they are summoned to a life always set under the cross. This is clear in one of Paul's most moving passages: 2 Cor 4:10–12:

> We always bear in our bodily existence the dying of Jesus, so that the life too of Jesus may be displayed in our mortal existence. For we as living persons are always being handed over to death for the sake of Jesus, so that the life of Jesus may also be displayed in our mortal nature. Thus death is at work in our case, but it is life for you.

*Second,* since the real issue under debate at Corinth was eschatological, that is, determined by the event celebrated by God's coming in Christ to remake the world and restore it to his saving purpose, Paul needed to assert what his understanding of the Christ event was. It entailed a paradoxical statement—and its paradox is perhaps the reason why the Corinthians misinterpreted it. They grasped one facet of truth and interpreted it in the light of their own hellenistic culture and enthusiastic experience as new converts. For them, all things had become new—a conviction Paul shared (2 Cor 5:17). He believed as passionately as any of his Corinthian friends that in Christ the decisive turning point in human history had been reached and life was radically transformed.

But he was realistic enough to qualify this unbridled confidence. Christians still live in a world of evil powers; they have to wrestle with temptation and to resist the downward drag of their being still "in Adam" (1 Cor 15:45-50); and their mortality must inevitably lead to death and dissolution, beyond which they cling to the hope of resurrection in a new bodily existence (1 Cor 15:38, 42-44; 2 Cor 5:1-10). This is the second member of the paradox which some of the Corinthians with their "realized eschatology" failed to grasp. Hence their denial of a future resurrection (1 Cor 15:12; cf. 2 Tim 2:17, 18). Paul insists on maintaining a tension in Christian living. The believers are already "in Christ" and part of the new creation (2 Cor 5:17); they have to live with the prospect of a final redemption still to come, and to order their lives on the principle of "as though" (1 Cor 7:29-31) by entering its life's moral responsibilities and challenges yet cognizant that this world will pass away.

# 2  PAUL'S APOSTOLIC SERVICE IN THEORY AND PRACTICE

Both letters open on the same note. While Paul's partner in ministry may not be the same—Timothy replaces Sosthenes in 2 Cor—the common theme is that of apostolic service. Paul presents himself in both letter openings as "an apostle of Christ Jesus." The other men are given the title "brother," i.e., fellow Christian and colleague. Only Paul is the apostle.

1. *Paul's Calling—from God.* It is clear that this designation stands at the center of both letters for several reasons. First, the appointment of the apostle is traced back to the purpose of God himself (1 Cor 12:28). For the establishing and good ordering of the church God's wisdom is seen in the gift of ministry. To be sure, all Christians have a part to play in building up the church (1 Cor 14:12) since all are gifted in one way or another (1 Cor 1:7; 12:4–11). But "the apostle" stands at the head of the list when Paul comes to consider the roll call of those summoned to particular ministry (see too,

Eph 4:11-16). The meaning of the word is that one is commissioned by the risen Lord (1 Cor 9:1) to proclaim the good news and lay the foundation which is identified as no less than Christ himself (1 Cor 3:10, 11). As a skilled master builder, Paul was conscious of his calling to this noble office, and faithfully acknowledges that Christ sent him . . . to preach the gospel (1 Cor 1:17). This was a vocation he accepted with all seriousness, regarding it as a calling not to be undertaken lightly but with due gravity and with a heavy sense of responsibility laid upon him (1 Cor 9:16). "Alas for me if I do not preach the gospel" echoes the conviction that he has a life-and-death mission to fulfill. The full implications of such a ministry are made clear in 2 Cor 2:15-17 where his apostolic work is pictured in contrast to that of his rivals, and the two types of ministry are set down in stark detail. Here is a short paragraph worth our close scrutiny:

> We are an aroma of Christ to God among those on the road to salvation—and among those on the road to ruin. Among those in the latter case [we are] a deadly fume that leads to death, but for those in the former a living-giving fragrance that leads to life. And who is adequate for this [kind of ministry]? For we do not go about adulterating God's message as our many [opponents] do. No, we speak as those who do so with sincerity, whose word is from God and given in the sight of God as servants of Christ.

The ministry of Paul is distinguished in two ways: (i) it calls forth a double reaction from the hearers. The book of Acts makes it clear that Paul's preaching did not permit his audience to remain in a fence-sitting neutrality once they had been confronted with the message of Christ. Now Paul explains to the Corinthians the nature of the choice, "rejection or response," which had accompanied his proclamation. To those who are destined to salvation the "word of the cross" (1 Cor 1:18) was a perfume of Christ, offering life in him (2 Cor 2:16). But to the mockers and the disobedient it came as a smell of death and doom. This contrast of fragrance as opposed to a fume that is lethal probably is drawn from the way the Jewish rabbis spoke of the law. The Mosaic law was likened to an aromatic medicine that proved health-giving to the righteous in Israel, but was fatal to the ungodly. Paul boldly takes over a Jewish use of picture language and applies it to the gospel he has been entrusted to announce.

(ii) The ministry in God's servant is marked by sincerity (2 Cor 2:17; see 1:12) in contrast to "many" who made "merchandise of the word." The latter is a strange phrase, probably a reference to certain contemporary religious teachers who put their preaching on a commercial basis by the constant flourish of the collection box. Paul had already made it plain (1 Cor 9:15-18) that he would have nothing to do with this type of mercenary practice, even when he had the privilege to be supported by his congregations. Here he mentions the only sort of accreditation worth having, in verse 17b: "as servants of Christ."

2. *His Self-Estimate.* Second, the reference to himself as numbered among those commissioned by God who are called to speak in Christ as in God's sight puts us on the track of how Paul saw himself as an apostle. One of the most revealing pieces of autobiography is in 1 Cor 15:8-11:

> Finally he appeared to me as to one abnormally born, as it were. I am the least of the apostles. I am not worthy to be called an apostle, because I persecuted the church of God. But what I am, I am by the grace of God; and his grace in my case has not been ineffective but I toiled more than all of them, yet not I, but the grace of God (working) with me. Whether then it was I or they (who

labored), this is what we proclaim and this is how you came to believe.

This personalized confession begins with Paul's claim to be an authentic witness of the risen Lord. While he never refers to the episode on the Damascus road as such, it seems evident that he has that event in view in his use of the words "he appeared to me." In spite of his previous record as a persecutor of the church, he was privileged to receive a heavenly vision that both forgave the past and set him on the road to a new future. The link term which alone explains how Saul of Tarsus became Paul the Christian leader is the grace of God. Though he ranks himself as a lowly person, as "the least of the apostles," he cannot deny how effectual the power of God has been in his life.

He makes a twofold claim in all humility, saying two things about his ministry simultaneously. On the one hand he concedes, "I am a special case. I labored more than all the apostles and have credentials"—such as his congregation at Corinth (1 Cor 9:2)—"to prove it." His work as a pioneer missionary (Rom 15:20; 2 Cor 10:12–16) is in view here. On the other hand, he draws back from the use of the personal pronoun. No sooner has he written "I" as in "I toiled" than he retracts it lest it should give a wrong impression. "Yet not I, but the grace of God" which was at work "with me."

In other words, he is conscious throughout his life's experience that while it would be false modesty to deny his "success," any achievement in church planting and growth is solely attributed to God's sovereign power. The same reminder has already been given in 1 Cor 3:6: "I planted, Apollos watered, but it was [only] God who gave the growth." C. K. Barrett appends a helpful and salutary comment.[1] "Merely to put a plant in the ground and pour water over it is nothing. It was not we, however, but . . . God who made [it] grow."

So Paul surveys his apostolic calling. He admits the unlikelihood (from a human point of view) of his ever becoming a believer, let alone an apostle. But then he sees in divine grace, which both drew him to God and empowers him for service, as 2 Cor 12:9 remarks, the sole explanation possible for such a transformation and such a record of exploits and endeavors. By God's grace (*charis*, the free favor of heaven to the undeserving) he became a Christian; and by the same grace he was enabled to fulfill his charge as an "apostle of Christ Jesus" to the Gentiles, a ministry he sought to magnify by humble dependence and thankfulness (Rom 11:13).

3. *Paul's Apostleship under Attack.* One feature of apostleship inevitably thrusts it into prominence in the Corinthian correspondence. At Corinth Paul's claim to be such a leader as a church planter and Christ's authorized representative was hotly disputed. The counterclaims of his rivals and opponents will need to be considered separately. The point we may make here is to note the way they viewed his apostolic calling. The catchword in 1 Cor 15:8 may be used as a starting point.

In the autobiographical section just examined Paul uses of himself the term *ektroma*, a word whose meaning is uncertain. The root idea is that of premature birth, an abortion, and so could be taken as "one hurried into the world before his time," as Barrett translates. In what way could this be said of Paul, or would he use it of himself? Perhaps there is a deliberate contrast between himself and the Jerusalem apostles (the "pillar" men of Gal 2:1-10) who had known Jesus in his earthly ministry. Paul, by contrast, had been "born without a full term of gestation," and had not known Jesus in his pre-resurrection days. This limitation may then have been used to make a denial of his equality with the Twelve to whose witness to the resurrection Paul had just appealed (15:5).

But the term *ektroma* is unnatural to express this idea, even if it is true that in 2 Cor 11:5 and 12:11 he will have occasion to claim that he is in no way inferior to the so-called "highest ranking apostles," meaning Peter or James or emissaries from the Jerusalem church. It has, therefore, been suggested that the term is one of abuse and was coined by Paul's enemies. They invented the term, meaning a malformed fetus and so a monster, and hurled it at him to discredit his apostolic rank. Perhaps they had in mind his lowly demeanor or his insignificance as a person (2 Cor 10:10), with a lack of theoretical skills and a simple style of preaching counting against him.

To support the latter we may refer to the extended discussion of Paul's preaching method in 1 Cor 1:17–2:5. He deliberately set his face against using the eloquent wisdom of the world in his public speaking, and came to Corinth "in weakness and in much fear and trembling" (2:3). His spoken utterance (*logos*) and his proclamation of the good news (the *kerygma*) were not offered in the persuasive words of (human) wisdom he confesses (2:4). The vital point to grasp is that it is the same reason he gives to justify both his lowly presence and his disdain of rhetorical finesse, namely so that the cross of Christ might not be emptied of its power with the consequence that if this happened the Corinthians' faith would rest on shaky ground (2:5). Yet Paul's person and proclamation were evidently the butt of criticism, and his opponents sought to exploit both to their own advantage.

There is, however, one further possibility for understanding *ektroma*. With a side-glance at Ephesians 3:8, "to me, who am less than the least of all Christians," it may be proposed that it was the Corinthians themselves who made playful allusion to Paul's name. *Paulos* in Greek is reminiscent of the Latin word for "little." Their quick wit seized on this link, and called him the "little one," which his enemies then used against him in contempt. In favor of this suggestion is that it links up with Paul's own continued thought in verse 9. There he turns the criticism to his own advantage:

"Yes, I am indeed the least [the same Greek root as in Eph 3:8] of the apostles"; he is an apostle for all people since he has seen the living Lord and has the indispensable qualification in being commissioned by him for his service (Rom 1:1, 5). It may be that he makes the same point in 1 Cor 4:3: "as for me it is a very little thing (same Greek word again) that I should be judged by you."

In the checklist of allegations brought against him at Corinth there was apparently the charge that he preached only an individualistic message, that is, his own version of the kerygma which, it was claimed, was at variance with the preaching of the original apostles. So Paul finds it needful to call in the evidence of the leaders to whom the risen Christ appeared. "Whether then it was I or they, this is what we proclaim and this is how you came to believe" (1 Cor 15:11). We may surmise, too, with some evidence drawn from 14:36–38, that a faction of the Corinthian congregation, perhaps led by a group of women prophetesses, were disputing Paul's role as the sole repository of divine truth, and claiming to have received fresh revelations from the Lord to contradict Paul's apostolic authority. Whatever the occasion, he is clear that he needs to establish the gospel he brought to Corinth as the epitome of God's saving truth. He goes about this task in several ways.

In 1 Cor 15:1–5 he presents the following lines of argument: (i) the "preached message" (15:1, lit. "the good news which I preached to you," which is a cumbersome piece of tautology in Greek but needful to enforce his point) has been validated in the readers' own experience (see 1 Cor 9:2). Paul can confidently appeal to the fact of Christian conviction, based on the way the Corinthians had received his message and were encouraged to stand firm in it.

(ii) The danger is that they should drift from the Pauline gospel, and Paul warns that this sad eventuality would only show that their initial faith was "in vain"—a possibility he does not seriously contemplate. (iii) Paul himself, though an apostle, was indebted to his predecessors and received from them the summary of the christological creed (in vv 3-5) which in turn he passed on to his hearers at the time of his first visit to Corinth (in Acts 18). (iv) Moreover this saving message is none other than the same gospel shared by other preachers and leaders in the early churches (v 11). His optimistic conclusion is thus reached. Whoever it was that brought the gospel—Paul in the first place, followed by subsequent visits of Peter and Apollos (1 Cor 9:5)—it is one and the same message. The creed expresses the common heritage of the faith, centered in a crucified and risen Lord, which all agree on, and in whose service Paul claims to have an unqualified place.

The sense of parity with the Twelve lies at the heart of this short but important section. The contents of the *kerygma* will be discussed later. It is enough now to note the way Paul's authority, clearly under fire, is defended by a series of reasoned statements drawn from personal experience, congregational endorsement, and the consensus of other leaders in early Christendom.

One other section (in 2 Cor 10:12-18) needs to be considered in the context of Paul's ministry. In the background is the accusation leveled against him that he had no right to be an apostle and certainly no sanction either from the Lord or from the leaders in the Jewish mission to come to Corinth in the first place. The allegation is probably touched on at 2 Cor 11:7 where the most likely interpretation of a difficult text is that the emissaries were claiming to be the sole representatives of Christ at Corinth, and so, by inference, insinuating that Paul's mission was invalid because he was not a true Christian, and so a phony leader.

He proceeds to counter this claim, and to offer his own understanding of what his apostleship meant in terms of keeping to the limits of the area designated to him as apostle to the

Gentiles. Some of the terms used are technical expressions and uncertain in meaning; but the chief thrust is clear. Paul, in typical fashion, cannot leave his argument without closing it in a tribute to the Lord who inspires all his service and to whom alone belongs the credit. We may reproduce some of these verses with a comment to draw out the implied sense.

> We do not have the effrontery to class or compare ourselves with some who recommend themselves. . . . We, however, will not boast beyond proper limits, but only within the sphere of service which God has assigned to us as our sphere, a sphere that reaches as far as to you. . . . We did not go beyond the proper limits by boasting of the work done by others, but we have the hope that as your faith continues to grow, so our work may, within the sphere we have, be greatly expanded among you. . . . For it is not the person who recommends himself who is approved, but the person whom the Lord recommends.

This difficult paragraph has a clear focus of vision, even if the details are obscure. Paul has in his sights the Jewish Christian proselytizers who were molesting Gentile church members and endeavoring to undermine his authority. They implied that Paul had no right to come to Corinth in the first place. He replies to the effect that if any preachers are "out of bounds" or "off limits" it is not he but those emissaries whose presence will appear at 11:4, 13–15. At Corinth, Paul justifiably claimed to be the human founder of the church (1 Cor 3:6). The Corinthians are the seal of his apostolic service (1 Cor 9:1, 2). In any case, the final arbiter is the sanction of the Lord to which he appeals in vv 17 and 18, as well as his divinely appointed destiny to be the herald of the gospel (Acts 9:15; 22:21; Eph 3:1, 2; 1 Clem 5:6, 7 for the later witness building on Rom 15:17–20).

*Paul's Apostolic Service in Theory and Practice*

*4. Apostle in Word and Life.* The apostolic ministry was expressed chiefly by Paul's spoken and authoritative words. Verbs such as "proclaim" and "declare" confirm this sense of importance he attached to his ministry as a spokesperson, called and commissioned by the heavenly Lord. He can sum up this aspect by citing the testimony of the Psalmist (Ps 116:10, LXX 115:1; 2 Cor 4:13) which joins together faith and the verbal utterance that flows from it. "We too believe and so we speak." Yet Paul knew that he was but a carrier or container in which the message was conveyed to his hearers. In a moving passage (2 Cor 4:7-12) he comments on the "treasure" of the good news committed to his charge, and proceeds to rehearse the way in which his own life is weak and expendable:

> But we have this treasure in clay pots, to show the preeminent power as God's not our own. We are hard pressed in every way, but not crushed by it; thrown into perplexity, but not left to despair; harassed, but not abandoned; knocked down, but not knocked out. (2 Cor 4:7-9)

"The earthen vessels" (v 7, RSV) refers to pottery jars used to carry possessions; or more likely they are to be understood as vessels for holding oil for use in a lamp. Many such containers have been found in recent archaeological digs at Corinth. Paul sees his own life as a bearer of the light of the gospel (2 Cor 4:4-6; Phil 2:16). The fragility of such cheap clay pots is only too obvious, and this fact emphasizes how little store Paul placed on his life. The series of paradoxical remarks in 4:8 and 9 is a memorable commentary and as we have reproduced the translation above, the play on words can be easily seen. The final paradox is summed up aphoristically in the sentence, "Thus death is at work in our case, but it is life for you" (v 12).

Not all at Corinth tended to see things this way. When Paul returns to the theme of the frailty and vulnerability of his apostolic service (in 2 Cor 11:23-29) it is clear that he is on the defensive. He cannot hide his record of suffering, hardship, and exposure to risk. Nor can he disguise the presence of "the thorn in the flesh" (2 Cor 12:7) which in some unexplained way was a hindrance to his ministry. All he can do is extol the grace of Christ that came to him in a surprisingly novel fashion (12:8) and confess that when he is at his weakest he is conscious of the divine power resting upon him.

The section, 12:7-10, is a memorable tribute to the paradoxical nature of the life of the apostle. In his extreme feebleness he was made aware of God's resources, and he came to learn the nature of the apostolic service. To those who were demanding "proof" (13:3) of his credentials and by implication criticizing Paul for lacking demonstrable signs and having no lordly bearing with its exemption from suffering, he points simply to the cross of Jesus (13:4; see 4:10) and to the lesson he has learned there. True apostolic authority derives from human weakness reinforced by divine strength and displayed in the signs mentioned in 12:12:

The marks of a [true] apostle were displayed [by God] among you in all persistence, [along with] signs and wonders and mighty works.

This is a verse that seems to incorporate what the Corinthians themselves judged to be infallible and convincing evidence of authentic Christian work. Paul quotes it back to them, adding significantly the phrase "with great perseverance" to make clear the point that his apostolic insignia were to be found not simply in outward display but more compellingly in the endurance which characterized the whole ministry of Jesus (Heb 12:2, 3) who has set the pattern of service for all time. In particular, Paul's patience with refractory people like the Corinthians is the surest sign of his calling from God!

Christian ministers and workers will continue to turn to Paul's self-portrait in the Corinthian letter to find there a model for their own service. Not all are called to be apostles. Indeed, Paul distinctly denies that this is a niche to be filled by more than just a few in the early church (1 Cor 12:29, "are all apostles?" expects the answer, no). Yet if the circle is a narrowly defined one and the office of apostle was restricted to that early generation of leaders who were the church's founding fathers and heroes (as Eph 2:20; Rev 21:14 imply), it still remains the case that Paul and his apostolic colleagues have left a pattern of ministry to be our incentive. It is based on the all-determinative paradigm of Jesus himself who was among his disciples as the servant-Messiah (Luke 22:27), and which beckons later ages of his would-be followers to accept as their own.

### Other titles

The term "title" is perhaps too pretentious. Paul's claim is certainly to be an apostle; but he does not explicitly refer to himself by any other self-designation with one or two exceptions. (a) The first exceptional case is in 2 Cor 3:6 where he writes of himself:

God gave us our adequacy to be servants of a new covenant, based not on the letter but on the Spirit.

Being a *servant* (lit. deacon) *of the new covenant* implied that he stood in a noble Old Testament succession. The new covenant is a reference to Jeremiah 31:31–34, an oracle in which the prophet foretells the dawn of a new era of God's dealings with his people. The old order based on a "written code" failed because the ancient people of Israel were faced with a standard they had no power to attain. For that reason it is concluded sadly that "the law kills" (3:6) and became a "dispensation of death" (3:7) which, in turn, led to "condemnation" (3:9). These strong terms can only mean that the law set a target or a perfect standard. But the Jewish people, like all nations, who were sinfully weak, were unable to rise to it.

The law, which Paul praised as "holy, righteous, good" (Rom 7:12, 14), had an honorable purpose, but it was only temporary. The illustration of the law's "parenthetic character" (as Gal 3:16-22 describes it) is seen in the way in which the glory of both the law (3:7, 11) and the lawgiver Moses (3:7), was only a passing one. The background is Exodus 34:25-35 which describes the splendor that shone from Moses' face, when he returned from communion with God. That radiance, however, faded in time and at length it disappeared just as a suntan does with us after a visit to a beach resort. From the lawgiver, Paul argues to that which he represented, namely the Jewish understanding of "salvation by law." Law whose glory was once historically a reality, is now fading away. Indeed, its day is over, and its impermanence has given way to that which has come to stay, namely the gospel (3:10, 11).

Of that good news, "the new covenant," Paul is a servant, and the glory of God once confined to Moses is open to all (3:18).

(b) Another exception is "minister of reconciliation" based on 2 Cor 5:18. He saw it as his life's work and mission to announce "the message of reconciliation" (5:19), as he declared that "God was in Christ reconciling the world to himself" (5:18). The calling to be an ambassador for Christ is stated in this context with the important observation:

[God] making his plea through us. We implore you, in Christ's behalf. Be reconciled to God!

Yet Paul's ministry of reconciliation has to be understood as more than a work discharged by public preaching, important as that side of his vocation was. He embodied in his whole demeanor and pastoral relationships the spirit of the good news he was charged to declare. His gospel was one of reconciliation; yet he lived out that message by his total ministry as a reconciling power and uniting the Corinthians to one another and to himself as their divinely appointed leader. We may see this facet of his apostleship on display in 2 Cor 7:8–13.

> Even if my letter hurt you, I do not regret it. Though I did regret it—for I see that letter hurt you for a while—now I rejoice, not that you sorrowed but that your sorrow led to repentance. For you experienced godly sorrow so that you suffered no loss through us. For godly sorrow produces repentance that leads to salvation and leaves no regret, but worldly sorrow leads to death. See what earnestness this godly sorrow has produced in you. . . . So then, when I wrote to you it was not on account of the offender, or of the offended, but on your account. . . . Because of this we are encouraged.

The historical setting of chapter 7 is worth an extended comment. Its line of thought and appeal go back to 6:11–13, which is one of the tenderest pieces in pastoral solicitude in the entire Pauline library:

> We have spoken freely to you, Corinthians, and opened our hearts wide. We do not withhold our affection from you, but you withhold affection from us. In return—as I speak to [my] children—you do the same to us.

The Corinthians are addressed as Paul's "beloved children" a sentiment recalling 1 Cor 4:14 and 15 in which he speaks of himself the "father" in the gospel. He became closely united to them as the one who first introduced them to Christ and witnessed their new life as children of God. To vary the metaphor, he was the "best man" who led the bride to the heavenly bridegroom and rejoiced at the nuptial ceremony (2 Cor 11:1, 2). Now, unhappily, they are estranged and alienated in their affections toward him. Even worse, they have crossed over the boundary line between the church where God's rule is acknowledged and the world in which the forces of evil are dominant. Hence they are referred to in 2 Cor 6:14–7:1 as having formed a liaison with unbelievers and have placed themselves under the dominion of Satan (called Belial, an epithet drawn from the intertestamental Jewish literature). Paul, however, cannot acquiesce with this situation, and appeals to these aggrieved children to quit their temporary aberration of hostility and come over to his side once more. Another impassioned plea (7:2–4) follows, with its ringing tones of confidence and optimism.

Make room for us [in your hearts]; we have wronged no one, we have ruined no one, we have taken advantage of no one. I do not say this to condemn you, for I have said previously that you are in our hearts; thus we die and live with you. I have more confidence in you: I take great pride in you. My encouragement is complete; I am overflowing with joy in all our distress.

The reason for such exuberant conviction that the Corinthians will indeed come back to their allegiance and be restored to Paul's loving care and favor is then rehearsed. On his part there is no strangeness or bitterness, though he did experience first apprehension and anxiety while he waited for Titus to return after the "tearful letter" (2 Cor 2:4, 5) had been delivered. Paul hastened to Macedonia from

Troas (2:13), not being able to settle even when a door of unexampled opportunity for evangelism lay wide open.

In Macedonia the two men rendezvoused, and the news was good. The letter had done its work (7:8–12; see 10:10) and Paul saw in the report of Titus an occasion for fresh joy and satisfaction (7:6). The heavy weight on Paul's pastoral heart had been lifted, and his spirit was free, as Titus met him with the excellent news that the Corinthian disaffection was over and their rebellion had been quelled.

More reasons for joy follow (7:5, 6). Not only has the church taken positive and courageous action, Paul's own estimate of the Corinthians themselves had been vindicated (as vv 4, 14 make clear). He had confessed to Titus that he believed, deep in his heart, that all would be well. Now he has not been put to shame; rather, what he said is "found to be true" (v 14). The work of reconciliation was—at least for the present—effective. And Paul's gospel message "be reconciled to God" (5:20) was shown to be powerful not only in causing sinners to return to God but in restoring an alienated congregation that had forsaken its loyalty to the gospel and deserted its first love for the messenger, Paul.

To complete the portrait of Paul the reconciler we need to fit in the earlier proposal of 2 Cor 2:5–11.

But if anyone has caused sorrow, he has caused sorrow not to me but in some measure—I mustn't put it too strongly—to all of you. The censure in question, which was inflicted on that person by the majority [of the church members] is enough for him, so that on the other hand, you should rather forgive and console him to prevent his being swallowed up by excessive sorrow. So I urge you, therefore, to affirm your love for this person. The reason I wrote to you was to see if you would pass the test and be obedient in everything. If you forgive anyone, I also do the same. For what I have forgiven—if indeed there was anything to forgive—it was done on your account in the presence of Christ, to prevent Satan from taking advantage of us; for we know well his designs.

Here he reviews the outcome of the visit he had paid, and focuses on his attitude to the one in the Corinthian assembly who had caused him pain. This person presumably was the individual who insulted him and fomented the trouble at Corinth, and he is also to be seen in the allusion in 7:12. The happy outcome of the painful letter (2:4) was to bring this person to his senses, and lead him to repentance (if, as is likely, he is to be included in the salutary response of 7:11).

Paul is generous to the point of bestowing his forgiveness on this person (2:10), as he summons the entire congregation to follow the example he has set: He will bear no grudge over injuries received, and sees that two extremes of attitude are equally to be condemned. The church must not be lax in handling moral problems (as is the case in 1 Cor 5:1-13 which is a different scene altogether, involving an arrogant transgression of the moral law); but it is just as destructive when the church refuses to grant pardon and restoration to the penitent sinner. Satan's cause is well advocated by either of these two polarities, as when the church is too tolerant of evil, on the one hand, and too rigorous in keeping the door of readmission shut tight, on the other.

Paul is seen in the intermediary role as reconciler in this historical interlude, a situation uniquely presented in his letter. The conclusion is irresistible: *What this man preached he practiced, and he was the living embodiment of the gospel of a forgiving Father who seeks and saves the lost.* The spirit in Jesus' parables in Luke 15 lives on in Paul's pastoral relations.

He has earned the right to set himself up as a role model (1 Cor 11:1: "Be imitators of me, as I belong to Christ"). 2 Cor 12:14 shows that he looked on the Corinthian people as his beloved children whom he cannot abandon, in spite of their waywardness and indifference to his love.

In summary, he was an apostle *par excellence*. But as Chrysostom reminds us, he was also a man, with tender human emotions and vulnerable to hurts and insults. Yet he overcame the natural tendency to fight back and to return injury with added vindictiveness. His entire relations with the Corinthian church exemplified his own teaching:

> Repay no one evil for evil, but take thought for what is noble in the sight of all. . . . Do not be overcome by evil; but overcome evil with good. (Rom 12:17, 21, RSV)

# 3   THE GOD AND FATHER OF OUR LORD JESUS CHRIST

To say we believe in God is to talk the language of theology. We are using the term "theology" in its strict sense to mean the understanding (*logos*) of God (*theos*). What is not implied is, of course, the notion that Paul had a highly developed doctrine of such matters as were to occupy the church's attention in later centuries. There is no hint in Paul's writings that he consciously drew upon a set of theological propositions to do with, say, the divine attributes or speculative concerns which seek to relate God and his eternal nature and purposes. The nearest we get to the latter is in Ephesians, a document which holds a unique place in the Pauline library of letters.

As far as the Corinthian correspondence goes, we find the apostle engaging in mostly practical and pastoral matters. His letters are a good example of "applied theology," to use H. Conzelmann's term.[1] But his understanding of God, while it may not be wrought out in any systematic way, still informs much of his writing to the church with its many-sided problems and needs.

Paul stood always in the tradition of his Jewish ancestral faith, inherited from the Old Testament Scriptures and interpreted by his upbringing as a Pharisee (Gal 1:13, 14; Phil 3:5, 6). In one place (2 Cor 11:22, 23) he offers a further sidelight on his Jewish background. Writing about the claims made by his opponents who came as rivals to Corinth he asks:

> Do they claim to be Hebrews? So am I. Do they claim to be Israelites? So am I. Are they Abraham's descendants? So am I. Are they Christ's servants? I am more one than they—even if I am out of my senses in claiming this. . . .

On the basis of this claim to have been brought up and educated as a pious Jew it may be further said that this training would have left an indelible mark on Paul's understanding of God. It is true that there is some dispute over the exact circumstances which surrounded his early days in Tarsus and Jerusalem (see Acts 23:3; 26:5, which may be read in more than one way). It is uncertain if Paul, in Luke's record, is tracing his boyhood upbringing to his life in Jerusalem as a pupil of rabbi Gamaliel or to Tarsus, the Cicilian city of his birth (Acts 21:39). What is more sure is that for Saul the ancestral traditions of his Jewish faith and practice were indescribably precious and influential. Though in one place (2 Cor 3:1–18) he is driven to deal critically with the centrality of Torah—the Jewish law and its interpretation—in the purposes of God, he reflects throughout his discussions in these two letters a deep appreciation of his Jewish heritage.

The central elements that would have been dominant in Saul's early life are three.

First, the confession of God as one goes back to the Deuteronomic creed, "Hear, O Israel, Yahweh our God is one" (Deut 6:4). This affirmation became embodied in the synagogue liturgy as the *shema*, a term taken from the opening verb, "hear." It marked the characteristic ethos and piety of Judaism in a way few religious watchwords do. Perhaps the nearest modern parallel is Islam's call of the mosque and minaret, "God is great."

Second, God has graciously made his will known in his law, Torah. Pharisaic Judaism held this divine revelation in high esteem, since it had been granted by God to Moses and transmitted to Joshua, and then to the elders of Israel and so on to the "great synagogue" (*Sayings of the Fathers*, 1:1: the opening sentence of this part of the Mishnah which brings together the sententious remarks of the Jewish sages over many centuries). The Torah, embodying both the written law of God entrusted to Moses and its oral interpretation committed to the men of the Jewish religious authority from the time of Ezra on, became so highly prized that it was given a kind of independent status. It is not always clear how the rabbinic language is to be understood. The praise of Torah (explicitly celebrated in Ps 119) is often excessive and couched in figurative writing. But there is no denying the power Torah came to possess and the hold it exerted on minds akin to Saul's in first-century Judaism. Paul, as a Christian, pays tribute to his upbringing: "the law is holy, and the commandment is holy and just and good" (Rom 7:12; see Rom 7:14, "the law is spiritual"). These convictions need to be borne in mind when we come to evaluate Paul's shift of perspective in 2 Cor 3 with its negative assessments of both, Torah regarded as the "letter that kills" (3:6) and the old covenant which is doomed to pass away (3:10, 11).

Thirdly, it is not surprising that since Torah is one of the chief pillars on which the world stands (*Sayings of the Fathers*, 1:2), it should be regarded as a "precious instrument"—in a phrase drawn from the rabbinic writings—signifying God's choice of Israel as his elect people. The nation is twice blessed by God: On the one side, Israel is claimed as Yahweh's special people bound to him by covenant deed and tie, and on the other, the people are told that God loves them. The token of that love is seen tangibly in the gift of Torah, which is a sign of Israel's privilege and destiny as a unique people. Torah became the visible expression of God's love in the covenant he graciously made with Moses and the people of the Exodus and in which they were bidden to enter by obedience. Paul never abandoned this fundamental conviction nor did he disown his Jewish past (Rom 9:1–5; 10:1), however much he might have to oppose some of his compatriots as he does in 2 Cor 11:13–15, and find fault with the "old covenant" in the light of his experience of Jesus Christ and the "new covenant" that came into the world with him (2 Cor 3:7–18).

The telling phrase that marks the transition from the old order to the new age is in 2 Cor 5:17: "if anyone comes to be in Christ, there is a new creation." Living as he did in the days of the new order in Christ, Paul is able to register some fresh understandings of God. Again, we may repeat it is not true that he jettisons his former beliefs in the God of his fathers, and denies the value of the covenant as a sign of divine grace (Rom 11:1, 2). Rather, he saw God's character in a new light. This is expressed in 2 Cor 4:4–6, which is important for one particular reason, namely, that it shows how Paul saw no incongruity in uniting the God of creation and the God of saving revelation in Christ:

> . . . the revealed splendor of the Gospel, that is the glory of Christ who is the image of God. . . . For it is the God who said, "Light shall shine out of darkness," who has shone in our hearts to illumine them with the knowledge of God's glory seen in the face of Christ.

Rather, what happened was that, with the coming of Christ as the final revelation of God, God now wore a human face and his person came into sharper focus. The scope of Paul's conclusion that God for him was henceforth known supremely in the knowledge he received of Christ may now be examined.

## God's name as Father

The tag that reminds us that as a person prays so that person's beliefs come to light is a sound one. We should therefore mark the way Paul's prayer language reflects his faith in God the Father-Parent. As a frontispiece to a discussion on the way he has been helped in his traumatic sufferings in Asia when he faced a deadly threat to his life (2 Cor 1:8–10), Paul strikes the chord of praise.

Blessed (be) the God and Father of our Lord Jesus Christ, the Father of mercies and the God of all encouragement. (2 Cor 1:3)

In point of fact, two reasons are given for the occasion of this outburst; they are developed in some detail in the opening section of the letter. First, he is full of thanks to God that in all the troubles that have weighed upon his spirit he has known the strength of God to carry him through. Suffering was Paul's destiny as the apostle to the Gentiles (Col 1:24; cf. Eph 3:13), and this "fate" was made known to him at the outset of his Christian life, according to Acts 9:15, 16. Yet Paul rests his faith in God as Father who is made known in our Lord Jesus Christ (see 2 Cor 11:31). He is called "the Father of mercies," a Jewish designation Paul may well have remembered from the synagogue prayers in his former years. It describes God as the Father who bestows mercy, who delights to hear his children's cry in their distress (Ps 145:18, 19). In this case, God's response was to afford his servant a full measure of "comfort" (Gr.

*The God and Father of Our Lord Jesus Christ*

*paraklesis*, which may be variously rendered "encouragement," "strengthening," or "solace")—a term which recurs as both noun and verb no fewer than ten times in the space of five verses.

The "comfort of God" is to be seen in the way Paul was able to trace a divine purpose in his tale of affliction borne for the gospel's sake. Thereby the cause of Christ and the gospel was advanced, and he was able to enter sympathetically into the experience of others (2 Cor 1:4) as well as, in a mysterious way on which Colossians 1:24 is the best commentary, see the purpose of God for his church and kingdom fulfilled (2 Cor 1:5-7). Later on, Paul will have reason to permit his readers to see more of what those hardships entailed (2 Cor 11:23-33). Here he is content simply to note the way in which God the Father sustained him by his *paraklesis* amid his daily life as a suffering apostle (see too, 2 Cor 4:16; 6:4-10).

The second reason for Paul's jubilant note is given at verses 8-11. In relating the experience of a crisis in Asia which exposes him to mortal danger he makes it plain that it was only by God's act of delivering mercy that he and his fellow missionaries had been saved (2:10). Yet God works by the prayers of his people, and Paul does not forget to tell that side of the story as well (2:11). Those who prayed to this faithful God (as 2 Cor 1:18 acknowledges him to be) are invited to share his gladness. Verse 11 is particularly interesting as a window into Paul's use of language. He coins a verb of fifteen Greek letters: "you help us by your prayers" (NIV) to convey three facets of his understanding of prayer. Prayer is at one and the same time a ministry involving work (*ergon*), cooperation (the preposition *syn*, "together") and support (the preposition is *hyper*, "under," "underneath"). So faith in God the heavenly Parent was a reality that expressed itself in prayer for assistance and timely help when imminent danger threatened, and Paul's congregations were invited to share such a ministry as an invaluable and cooperative support offered to Paul's mission.

In this instance prayer was effectual in releasing divine power which in turn resulted in an intervention that brought release from danger. The allusion to "so terrible a death" (1:10, Moffatt) suggests a life-threatening prospect which stared him in the face. Now he thankfully records how the heavenly deliverance came, though the details are not disclosed. Perhaps 1 Cor 15:32—"if as a mortal man I fought with beasts at Ephesus, what advantage would it be to me, if the dead are not raised?"—refers to the same encounter. Some interpreters view the phrase about "fighting with beasts" as a literal and certain fact, and suggest that Paul was indeed condemned to the arena. Then he must have been rescued, like Daniel, by a marvelous intervention. After all, he did live to tell the tale!

The phrase, rendered literally "as a man" (*kata anthropon*), must mean more than "as a human being," since how else could Paul have been exposed to death? An alternative meaning is "after the manner of men [who have no hope of resurrection]"; then Paul is pointing to the hopeless state he would have been in if he had had no prospect of resurrection to cheer him in his trials when he faced death as his daily experience (1 Cor 15:31: "I die every day").

A third option is that taken by the RSV which translates "humanly speaking," suggesting that he is speaking in metaphorical language and perhaps with a proverbial expression for some deadly—but human—opposition he knew at Ephesus (such as that mentioned in 1 Cor 16:8, 9). There is also the historical question whether Paul as a Roman citizen would have faced the danger in capital punishment in a provincial center like Ephesus. If he were allowed to plead his citizenship rights, the law protected him from such a fate (as it did in the different but equally threatening circumstance of Acts 25:6–12). There are some other possibilities of interpretation,

*The God and Father of Our Lord Jesus Christ*

namely that Paul is referring to an event that seemed likely to occur but never did happen. Yet verse 30 stands against this view since Paul was really in danger. Or else the life-threatening event that he faced in Ephesus is to be identified with the situation of Acts 19:23–41; yet that account hardly suggests a serious threat to his very life, and the idiom of "fighting with [wild] beasts" seems hyperbole in that case.

We may never know the real cause of Paul's extremity. It looks to be tied in with the "death sentence" of 2 Cor 1:9, 10, and may also connect with the grim prospect in a life-or-death "choice" in Phil 1:20–24; 2:17. The most we can safely conclude is that somewhere in the Asian province, probably at Ephesus, during his three-year stay there (Acts chs 19 and 20) he faced a foreboding situation in which the end of his life seemed close and by some judicial verdict he was under sentence, with little hope of reprieve. He was, he says, like a man doomed to the arena with no prospect of escape and no hope, except that for him as a believer in the God and Father of our Lord Jesus Christ, "who raises the dead" (2 Cor 1:9) divine help was implored and granted. But—and this is the point of Paul's argumentative appeal to the Corinthians—even before the deliverance came he had the assurance of "life after death" such as had sustained the Maccabean martyrs (see Dan 3:16, 17; 2 Macc 7:14; cf. Heb 11:35), and his confidence was not misplaced. God heard and answered his plea.

Side by side with this moving episode and its sequel we need to set, as a counterpoint, the dialogue of 2 Cor 12:1–10. The background here, to be sure, is not the same mortal peril as in the earlier text; but the "thorn in the flesh" did pose a challenge to Paul's faith and did place a limitation on his missionary service. The real problem, however, lay elsewhere, if 12:7a is taken in all seriousness. It was to save him from being puffed up with pride that God in his infinite wisdom and providence allowed the handicap to remain.

The "thorn in the flesh" (12:7, KJV) is a curious phrase which is capable of at least two meanings. (i) It is clear that it was inherently evil as Satan's emissary, and (ii) it came to him as an affliction, intended to "torment" him. Some definite weakness which restricted Paul's missionary service is apparently in mind, and "in the flesh" (te sarki) is most naturally understood as a physical problem, though sarx ("flesh") does also have a common meaning in Paul of a human inclination to evil; and that sense could conceivably be true here. It was to prick the bubble of inordinate pride that the thorn was permitted, and as a consequence Paul was kept humble. But verse 9b, "Therefore I will most gladly boast in my weaknesses," reads strangely as a deduction from this way of identifying the reason behind the thorn. We should conclude that it was a distressing physical liability from which he sought to be free.

The answer that came in response to his petitioning prayer for its removal was a paradoxical one. The thorn remained, but its sting was drawn, and its limiting purpose (so designed by Satan) was turned to good effect. The bane became a blessing; and, as one preacher comments, through God's "no" Paul learned to hear God's "yes."

We may trace a threefold way in which this experience contributed to Paul's understanding of God and his ways with his servants:

(a) By this evil which was permitted to remain, God's purpose was achieved in keeping Paul in humble dependence on him (12:7, "in order that I should not become conceited"—which is one of the key phrases in the dramatic autobiography). Paul was continually reminded of his frailty and finitude, and he turns such a reminder to telling effect in his debate with the opponents whose lordly ways and overbearing disposition (see 11:20, 21) were regarded as the badge of apostolic authority.

(b) The divine oracle which promised, "My grace is sufficient for you, for [my] power is fulfilled in [human] weakness"

(12:9) makes it evident that Paul came to experience Christ's presence and power in a new way. In the hard school of discipline and suffering he learned lessons of trust and reliance on God's strength which presumably he could never have known except in this bitter frustration. As only those who are self-confessedly ignorant can really be taught, so only those who know their true need will find in Christ the supply and fulness of God, as 1 Cor 1:20-31; 2:12-16 illustrate. The Corinthians with their proud display of intellectual prowess and confidence in their native ability could not appreciate how Paul's gospel and apostolic service were built on the power of love (1 Cor 8:1) and centered on a Jesus who was crucified in weakness (2 Cor 13:4). The very idea of a suffering and sick apostle to them seemed a contradiction in terms, and a charismatic healer who could not heal himself stood self-condemned in their eyes. They needed to hear from Paul that it is God's power, not human bravura, that authenticates the gospel.

(c) Several interpreters, led by Sir William Ramsay[2] in a former generation, have found in this incident on the thorn in the flesh an indication that Paul was an habitually sick man, attacked often (Ramsay proposed) by malarial fever, which is then identified as the nature of "the thorn." In this way Ramsay was able to explain Paul's short stay in the lowlands and unhealthy climate of Pamphylia (Acts 13:13), and his swift journey, beyond the Taurus Mountains, to the more bracing climate of Galatia. Gal 4:13 and 14 was taken to confirm this view, and to illustrate the truth that illness, instead of closing a door on service for Christ, actually prompted Paul to venture forth and to claim the Galatian towns for the gospel. This reading of the evidence is necessarily speculative, but it is suggestive, and could well be true.

But we have to come back to the candid conclusion that the identity of the thorn is a mystery; and perhaps that is providentially so, that all sufferers for the gospel's sake may claim some affinity with the ailing apostle. What should not be in question is Paul's understanding of the character of God as good and trustworthy whether the answers to prayers are affirmative (as in 2 Cor 1) or—as we say—negative (as in 2 Cor 12). Yet "negative" is not the correct term, as we have observed. Even when God's power was concealed in Paul's persistent weakness, the essence of the gospel was unfolded and wonderfully displayed. More particularly the parenthood of God is revealed in the various ways that prayers are answered.

### God as Father and Son

Paul's belief in one God was never compromised, given the enduring Jewish convictions he retained. He makes this clear in 1 Cor 8:4-6. We cannot be certain in this passage which has a creedal ring to it how much he is quoting from the Corinthians and at what point he is commenting on beliefs held in common. "We know that an idol is nothing at all in the world, and that there is no God but one" (v 4) looks to be a quoted statement, with which Paul partly agreed and to which he partly took exception (see 1 Cor 10:19, 20). The monotheism of the second statement, "God is one," is clearly Paul's belief as well, since it reappears in Gal 3:20, and in 1 Tim 2:5 in different settings.

The issue in 1 Cor chs 8 and 10 is the problem of idol foods. The church was evidently in two minds over the propriety of eating food (especially meat) that had been formerly used in temple worship in contemporary hellenistic-Roman religions. Only a portion of that meat was consumed in the sacrificial offerings to the gods; the rest, once formally presented to the deity, was offered for sale in Corinthian butchers' shops.

The question posed for Paul's pastoral response is this: Was the Christian housewife at liberty to buy and use this meat, which was often the best "cut" on display in the store (1 Cor 10:25) since all sacrificial foods had to be free from blemish? The "strong" among the Corinthian believers replied that she was able, because after all, idols were non-existent and so couldn't contaminate food. The alternative (mainly Jewish) view was that the housewife-shopper should refrain because idolatry did cast a spell over food, thus making it unclean and unfit for human consumption by believers.

The dilemma facing the church in a pagan society is illustrated in this way, and Paul shows some wise pastoral discretion, especially when the issues involved move from theological belief to practical matters such as whether or not Christians were at liberty to take a meal in a neighborhood temple (1 Cor 8:10). The latter question will be considered when we address Paul's ethical teaching. For the present it is enough to note how his belief in God is the starting point for his applied theology.

Paul seems to be wanting to make two statements—not easily harmonized—at the same time. First, God's sole existence is affirmed, consonant with his Jewish and Christian tradition. Second, he sensed the danger presented by the demonic and the power that is exerted over sensitive minds (1 Cor 10:18-22).

He grants that gods and goddesses do have an influence, since the threat of coming under alien influences is very real—at least to some of his converts. He writes as a Christian believer who must not consciously acknowledge any power save that of God; for the principle involved see 1 Cor 6:12: "everything is permissible for me," which is the Corinthian slogan as he quotes it, then adding the comment, "but I will not be mastered by anything." For that reason the gods are dubbed "so-called" (in 1 Cor 8:5), even if they did command a following and their existential reality is conveyed in such phrases as "the cup of demons," "the table of demons" (1 Cor 10:21). Yet Paul is too much a monotheist to grant a real existence to any dualistic divine power, set up in rivalry to the only God of Old Testament and Christian faith. So he quickly qualifies his concession: "yet' to us there is but one God the Father, from whom all things come and for whom we exist," with the distinctively Christian assertion added, "and there is but one Lord, Jesus Christ, through whom all things come and through whom we exist" (1 Cor 8:6).

It has long been recognized that here we have the first makings of the Christian confessional formula, covering Articles I and II of the later creed. Believers join the belief in God the Father and God the Son as the two persons in what later developed into full-blown binitarianism, that is, the confession of the Father and the Son as equal members of the godhead.

In these epistles the mutual relationships within the Christian godhead are not systematically explored; rather they lie back-to-back. For example, in his rebuke to party divisions and the setting up of apostolic figures as centers of loyalty Paul retorts, "All things are yours" including the prized names of Apollos and Peter and himself (1 Cor 3:21, 22). Even those leaders' names are only significant as they are seen as workers together with God (1 Cor 3:5-9; 2 Cor 6:1) and servants of Christ the Lord (2 Cor 4:5). Life and death, this world and the age to come, present and future—the list recalls the wording of Rom 8:38 and 39—are all held in the mighty grip of God whose promise is that all history serves his eternal purpose for the church. "You belong to Christ, just as Christ belongs to God" is Paul's final summing up. The note of equality within the divine community of the Father and the Son, evident in 1 Cor 8:6 is now matched by the element of subordination that makes Christ not inferior to God but occupying a position given him by God. His title is then of lordship which is conferred by divine favor (Phil 2:9-11) which includes Christ's role as head of the universe (1 Cor 15:25) and the church (1 Cor

1:2). At present he reigns in a mediatorial kingdom and awaits the day when as the risen Lord all his foes will be subject to him and "put under his feet" (1 Cor 15:25 citing Ps 8:6). At the Parousia Christ's kingdom which is parallel with the church age and the present Regnum Christi will come to its appointed close; then Christ will surrender his kingdom to God whose final kingdom, the Regnum Dei, will be all-inclusive (1 Cor 15:28).

Paul is once more caught in the dilemma of his own faith. As a faithful Jewish pietist he can tolerate no rivalry to God, no dualism that sets up a split within the divine nature. Hence the Son will at the last take his place within the sole monarchy of God, a description Paul calls the Son's becoming "subject to him who put everything under him" (1 Cor 15:28). The key word is "subject," which in the Bible denotes not submission or slavery, in the popular sense of the term, but as the English word properly implies, "being placed under" and fulfilling one's role by sharing in it, as 1 Pet 2:13 following Rom 13:1 well illustrates.

At the same time Paul is driven by all he knows of Christ as the resurrected Lord and the head of a new humanity (1 Cor 15:20, 21) to ascribe divine honors to him. In 2 Cor 3:12–18 he sets the present-day reader a conundrum with his assertion that "the Lord is the Spirit" (3:17). Apparently he means to link the Lord (who is Jesus) with the God of the Old Testament to whom Moses turned for communion and transformation. The link factor is the Spirit who does for the Christian believer what Yahweh's glory did for Moses. Their unveiled faces are irradiated by divine splendor as they "behold" (NIV marg. has "contemplate") the glory of Christ and are changed. Here is one of the clearest places in Paul of what has been called his practice of "eschatological exegesis" which puts the risen Jesus on a par with Yahweh in the Old Testament, and sees Jesus as eminently worthy of divine worship and obedience.

It is natural for Paul then to conclude that what God did in old times for his ancient people, he does today in his Son. Significantly, as with the church father Athanasius, the issue is one of redemption. It is in the soteriological exposition of 2 Cor 5:17–21 that he reaches the most explicit expression on the unity of purpose that binds together the Father God and Jesus Christ. We should first offer a rendering of those magnificent statements wherein Paul's gospel of salvation and reconciliation is unfolded.

If anyone comes to be in Christ, there is a new creation; the old order has gone, to be replaced by the new [in every way]. And this new order in all respects is God's doing, who reconciled us to himself through Christ and has given us the ministry of reconciliation. Its terms are that in Christ God was reconciling the world to himself, not charging humankind's offenses against them. And he has entrusted us with the message of reconciliation. We are then ambassadors for Christ, with God making his plea through us. We implore you, in Christ's behalf. Be reconciled to God! God appointed him (who was without any acquaintance with sin) to be a sin-offering on our behalf, that in him we might become the righteousness of God.

The pivotal phrase, for our purpose in this strictly theological section, is v 19. The Greek is capable of being understood in a variety of ways (to be considered in a later chapter). What is clear is that a single purpose unites God and the one in whom his presence was made known both to reveal his desire to win the sinful world back to himself in reconciliation and to execute that plan by becoming one with humanity in its sin in order to bring God's saving power, his "righteousness," to bear on human relationships. No hint of a division within the godhead as though Father and Son were two separate "agents"—one intentionally acting, the other unwillingly passive—is to be seen here. Rather, a singlemindedness of plan and its outworking is to be noted. Much mischief in theories of the Atonement has resulted from pitting the Father against his son Jesus, thereby making a mockery of the very unity Paul's words celebrate.

## God as Trinity

Once more we should remind ourselves that "Trinity" is a later technical term, employed to define the way the Christian godhead was conceptualized—and experienced. Yet if the test is one of experience, it could be plausibly argued that the roots of trinitarian belief-based-on-experience go back to Paul and the Corinthian correspondence. Three passages stand out preeminently: (a) 2 Cor 1:20-22:

To all the divine promises, however many they are, the "Yes" is in him; and that is why it is through him that we say our Amen to God for his glory. Now it is God who confirms both us and you in our relationship to Christ. He has anointed us, set his seal upon us, and imparted the Spirit to us as a pledge.

Here in an unself-conscious way Paul sets the purpose in God, made actual in Christ who confirms all his promises in the Old Testament, alongside the manner in which truth becomes realized in experience. With a play on words, it is in the "Anointed one" (=Christ) that Christians are "anointed" in the sense of being set apart for God's use and service (cf. Acts 10:38). The outward sign, probably baptism, answers to the inner experience of the Spirit in an act of "sealing" which repeats the idea of setting apart for ownership and possession (see NIV).

Thus the three "persons" of the Christian godhead are brought into the picture in a statement on the different sphere of operations which each one fulfills. The Father is the originator and chief actor; he works in human lives through Christ whose destiny is somehow shared by his people who own his name (as "Christians," which became their later designation and title); and it is by the Spirit that God comes to live in human lives, offering the first installment (*arrabon*) of the final salvation whose reality is already known by its initial token. When it is recalled that *arrabona* is in modern Greek the word for an engagement ring, the sense will be immediately clear. The Holy Spirit, given to believers now, is the assurance that God's work of salvation will be ultimately completed, just as the engagement ring is a pledge that a wedding date is to be set and the marital union made real (see 2 Cor 5:5).

Each "member" of the Trinity is thus accorded a role— in appointing the means of salvation, becoming the agent through whom that salvation is actualized, and applying its benefits in human experience. Interestingly, this pattern became the format followed by the later christological and ecumenical creeds, beginning with the Apostles' Creed, which was a baptismal formulation adopted by the church at Rome in the mid-second century.

(b) The same appeal to living experience underlies the more elaborately worded passage in 1 Cor 12:4-6. The general theme is set by the apostle's confidence that, though the gift of the Spirit is one and is evidenced most plainly in giving voice to the confession "Jesus is Lord" (12:3), the gifts of the Spirit are diverse and manifold. Paul will conclude (at 12:11), restating the fact that the Spirit acts in sovereign power whether to give or withhold particular *charismata*, i.e., gifts intended to build up Christ's body, the church. In the interlude of 12:4-6 he shows how the acts of the Holy Spirit, which are really related to God's bestowal of *charismata*, are set in a structure that can only be described as trinitarian or at least triadic. The arrangement of his thought is as follows:

> The same Spirit . . . yet different kinds of gifts; The same Lord (Jesus Christ) . . . yet different kinds of service; The same God (the Father) . . . yet different kinds of operations.

The three key themes—"gifts" (*charismata*), "services" (*diakoniai*) and "operations" (*energemata*) are linked, and it is difficult to draw firm lines of distinction. The most that can be safely concluded is that *charismata* are the ways in which divine grace (*charis*) becomes actual and concrete, to use E. Käsemann's expression.[3] The second term refers to ministries in which the gifts become real in practice; the last word suggests outworking with definite results.

What Paul seems intent on stressing is the manifold variety in such gifts that proceed indiscriminately from the several members of the godhead. All the "persons"—Father, Son, Spirit—combine to make possible a set of "distributions" (*diaireseis*) to the members of the church—a fact of giftedness Paul had recognized at the outset of the letter (1 Cor 1:7). Thus the members of the divine reality called God are for Paul functional in granting gifts which in turn are intended to be employed for the triune glory.

(c) 2 Cor 13:14 presents its own complications of syntax and meaning, especially regarding the phrase "the fellowship of the Holy Spirit." The question is, did Paul mean the fellowship imparted by the Spirit or the fellowship which believers enjoy with the Spirit? The verse can be taken in either way, though the balance of scholarly opinion has been in favor of the second option, following the pattern set in 1 Cor 1:9: "God is to be trusted, by whom you were called into fellowship with his son, Jesus Christ our Lord" and 1 Cor 10:16: "the cup of blessing, over which we give thanks, is it not a [means of] fellowship with the blood of Christ?" See too 2 Cor 1:7, "we know that, as you share in the sufferings, so also you share in the encouragement."

On the other hand, there is no denying that "the grace of the Lord Jesus Christ and the love of God" mean the grace made known in Jesus Christ and the love that God has for his people, so it is natural to expect the third phrase to run: the fellowship created by the Holy Spirit. The relevance of this sense to the context is seen in the way Paul closes the benediction by asking that such blessings may be "with you all," a term that suggests that the whole church is in view. Finally, he has already (in 1 Cor 12:13) paid tribute to the Holy Spirit as the agent of the church's unity, and it is fitting that to a divided congregation he would wish to appeal for a true *koinonia* made possible by the work of the Holy Spirit. There is perhaps a polemical undertone to this concluding verse of a lengthy section (2 Cor chs 10–13) which has been defensive and combative throughout.

The latest full study on this question, by J. Hainz, makes an interesting point, namely that there is possibly no need to set a hard-and-fast line between the two rival interpretations.[4] The primary focus, Hainz remarks, is on "the fellowship of the church" made possible by the common share which all believers have in the Holy Spirit.

In this finale Paul breathes the spirit of prayer. He calls down on the church at Corinth the blessing of the entire godhead. The opening reference to "the grace of the Lord Jesus Christ" recalls 2 Cor 8:9 with its appeal to the condescension and love that brought the Lord of glory to earth and to his destiny as the church's redeemer. In that Incarnation the Father's love is revealed, which matches "the love of Christ" in 5:14. In both cases it is the same love that Father and Son demonstrate for the church and its service to the world. Thirdly, the *koinonia* of the Holy Spirit is that bond that unites believers both in mutual regard and harmony (see

2 Cor 13:11, 12) and in the common life that derives from the life-giving Spirit (2 Cor 3:6, 17, 18) whom Christians have received at their initiation into Christ's body (1 Cor 12:12, 13) and as a down payment on their future and final redemption (2 Cor 1:22) and resurrection (2 Cor 5:5).

The entire Christian godhead is thus in Paul's mind and is invoked in this memorable way. Divine resources are made available to reinforce the apostle's appeal for unity and amity.

# 4 THE GRACE AND GLORY OF OUR LORD JESUS CHRIST

At the heart of the gospel Paul brought to Corinth was the person of Jesus Christ, "the Son of God . . . whom we preached among you" (2 Cor 1:19). It is true that such a statement needs to be examined with some caution. For one thing, Paul has no speculative interest in christology or any set "doctrine of Christ." His presentation of who Jesus was and is related directly to his own experience as a person to whom the Lord of glory appeared in a life-directing manner, as 2 Cor 4:4–6 describes the "conversion" of Paul. Recent studies put at the center of Paul's entry on new life the awareness he had of God's glory shining in the person or face of Jesus; and the paragraph in 4:4–6 holds an important place in Paul's autobiography. We must examine that section again.

Yet, as a counterpoint to what was just said, Paul was no innovator who created a "doctrine of Christ" solely out of his own experience. Nor did he receive it in a heavenly

*The Grace and Glory of Our Lord Jesus Christ*

vision unrelated to the ongoing life and community of those who were his Christian predecessors or contemporaries. The evidence in 1 Cor 15:1–5 is crucial. It supports the view that Paul was indebted to his forerunners in Christ— to whom he refers almost casually in Rom 16:7 as being "in Christ before me"—for the understanding of an early Christian credo or statement of belief that he in turn passed on to the Corinthians:

> I make known to you, brothers, the good news which I proclaimed to you. You received it; you stand firm by it; through it you are being saved, if you hold fast to the message which I proclaimed to you—unless you believed in vain. I handed on to you, then, as a priority what I also received: that Christ died for our sins, in accordance with the Scriptures; that he was buried; that he was raised on the third day in accordance with the Scriptures; and that he appeared to Cephas; then to the Twelve.

The churches of the New Testament period were confessing companies of men and women. By "confessing" we mean that they cherished and were committed to a body of teaching (however rudimentary and situation-oriented it may have been initially) that was believed to express the substance of the saving message.

Only on the assumption of such a teaching that was accepted as normative can we account for two attested facts in early Christianity. One is the consciousness of the church's being a distinct entity in the world over against both Jews and Gentiles (1 Cor 10:32). The other factor is the church's missionary goal which, under the influence of Stephen and his followers, and then Paul, showed a concern to proclaim the good news to all people, irrespective of ethnic origin. The main outline of that creed, which was essentially christological is seen in the passage just cited. There are several tell-tale signs that stamp it as a "fixed" formula of Christian—specifically christological—belief: (i) the fourfold repeated "that" (*hoti*) to introduce each line in vv 3-5; (ii) the vocabulary is unusual for Paul who does not normally write "in accordance with the Scriptures" in his preference for "as it is written" (twenty-nine times) to refer to the Old Testament; (iii) the lines run in parallelism and use the idioms in Isa 53, which is a favorite Old Testament chapter in other creedal passages (e.g., Rom 4:24, 25); and (iv) most decisively the emphatic preface in 15:3 tells us that Paul is quoting what he in fact "received" and in turn "passed on" to the Corinthians at the time of his initial evangelism in their city. To those generally accepted beliefs he alludes in v 11, as he calls on the other apostolic preachers for support.

Paul's invoking the consensus shared with other leaders is deliberate. He is on the defensive against the Corinthians who challenged his apostleship and no doubt alleged that he was an inferior apostle—or even that he was no true apostle (as 2 Cor 10:7 implies). But here is also another side to Paul's strategy in building his case on a recited creed. One of the chief problems at Corinth was the influence of teachers who were claiming to be exponents of a message they had privately received. This is clear from 1 Cor 14:36: "Was it from you that God's message went out? Did it reach you alone?" This is the literal rendering which the RSV expands to bring out the implied thought:

What! Did the word of God originate with you or are you the only ones it has reached?

From this translation we may catch the tone of Paul's indignant rebuttal. Against those who thought that they had a "corner" on God's truth, and that the special revelation had come to them as highly favored individuals Paul retorts that this is not so. He brought the gospel in the first place. He was indebted to others who instructed him. And his message was consonant with that of the leading apostolic figures, especially the "highest-ranking apostles" (2 Cor 11:5; 12:11).

Thirdly—and again we need to interject a caution—the presence of an agreed statement that expressed the essence of Christian faith did not make it impossible for some to entertain notions that Paul judged greatly in error. One place in the Corinthian letters offers a clear example of wrong-headed christological views—2 Cor 11:4—and to that passage also we must revert. What made that rival message so dangerous, in Paul's eyes, was that it was being introduced to the Corinthians as a "different gospel" by those who came with a "different spirit." More seriously still, it was not an alternative version that Paul could tolerate alongside his understanding of the saving message, as evidently he was resigned to having to live with the preaching referred to in Phil 1:15-18. The chiefest element in this presentation as it was brought on to the scene at Corinth was that it preached and exemplified "a rival Jesus whom we did not proclaim." The outstanding difference from the Pauline message lay in its christology, and that novelty raised for Paul a warning signal, which prompted his fierce denunciations in 11:13-15.

These people are bogus apostles, workers of deceit, masquerading as Christ's apostles. . . . Satan himself masquerades as a messenger of light. It is no great surprise, then, if his servants too masquerade as servants of righteousness. Their fate will be what their deeds deserve.

So Paul's proclamation of Jesus Christ at Corinth, while adapted to meet the needs of the hour, rested firmly in the accepted traditions he shared with other prominent apostles and went back to an early "creed." At the same time it was challenged by freewheeling missionaries who appeared on the scene to offer a "rival" christology. Paul is at pains to expose and refute this, since (evidently) it ran counter to his teaching on the person and place of Jesus Christ and was being offered to the Corinthians in a way that effectively opposed Paul's understanding of both Christian ministry and the Christian life. It is time now to review Paul's teaching on these themes.

1. Since we have just mentioned Paul's debt to his past, presumably the Jewish Christians who were located in Jerusalem and Antioch, it is fitting to recover from the obscurity of their language one of the most interesting christological allusions. 1 Cor 16:22 runs:

If anyone does not love the Lord, let him be anathema. Maranatha.

Maranatha is clearly not a Greek word, yet Paul is able to leave it untranslated in his letter written to Greek-speaking, Greek-reading people. The only explanation for this is that he expected his readers to know what the Aramaic word stood for, most likely because it was already part of their vocabulary of worship. A parallel case would be with present-day liturgical and worship words which we use without stopping to translate them in English, such as *Amen, Hallelujah, Hosanna*.

The puzzle with Maranatha is rather with the way the word is to be divided: whether *maran atha*, meaning "The Lord comes," or *marana tha* "Our Lord, come!" The second choice is most likely to be correct, and thereby it confronts us with a prayer of invocation as the (risen) Lord is invoked in worship.

A final question has to do with the setting, and again we have a choice. Either, the term is eschatological in bidding the worshiper to anticipate with joyful acclaim the Parousia of Christ, or, set in a service of the Lord's supper meal (1 Cor 11:17–34), it expresses a hope and confidence that the presence of the living Lord will come to greet those who take the bread and the cup "in remembrance of" him, i.e., to make him real to faith. Either way the cry is an utterance of expectant faith in the presence of the risen Christ, whether at the end of the age or at his table which is also an anticipation of the Parousia (1 Cor 11:26: "until he comes"). Whether eschatological or eucharistic in setting, the invocation is directed to one whose title is Lord (mar, which recalls the Jewish use of a divine title used of Yahweh) and whose living presence in the present is at the heart of both the church's sacrament and the church's hope for the future. A solitary watchword like Maranatha is a window through which we glimpse the early Christians at their devotions; it is also a precious datum of their belief in the present Lordship of one whom they had begun to associate with their covenant God, if (as is very likely) Maranatha takes us back to an early Palestinian or Syrian community of Jewish-Christian believers whose language quickly passed over into cosmopolitan centers such as Corinth.

2. The present reign of Christ is the theme of 1 Cor 15:23–28, a section whose centerpoint has at v 25: "he must continue his reign"—the tense is present—"until he has placed all his enemies under his feet."

The present tense of Paul's infinitive verb, "to reign," is distinctive, though heralded by the use of the perfect tense in v 20: "But in reality Christ has been raised from the dead" where the verb, grammatically important, speaks of a past event with continuing consequences that spill over into the present. There is both a "pastness"—he was raised on the third day (1 Cor 15:4)—and a present significance to the Lord's resurrection. Paul's thought goes a step further in v 25 which highlights the contemporary rule of Christ. Since these two vv (20, 25) make some emphatic pronouncements answering the present Lordship of

Christ, we should inquire why Paul found it needful to write as he did.

Up to this point in his discussion he has been somberly negative in pointing to humanity's involvement in Adam's loss. He indicates the sentence of death that has become universal as humanity's condition (15:21). Yet the resurrection of Jesus has spelled the dawn of a new chapter in world history, involving two aspects: (i) "Death," which is often thought of in Jewish writings as a king or a kingdom that holds tyrannical control over its subjects, is now subject to the power of the risen Lord. The iron grip that death had imposed on the human race, from Adam onward, has been broken, and death's kingdom has been despoiled.

Yet believers like all of humankind have to die, and death remains the "last enemy" (15:26) whose destruction awaits the future Parousia, when all Christ's enemies will be finally brought into submission. So Paul checks the unwarranted conclusion that evidently some at Corinth had drawn. They were exulting in Christ's present reign as though it was a reality all on its own (1 Cor 4:8). Paul agrees with the statement that Christ's rule has begun, but its power is not uncontested and awaits a fulfillment in the future when "all his enemies" are set "under his feet," with the last enemy clearly identified as death. At first sight it looks as if that subjection has already taken place (indeed, the hymnic passage in Eph 1:21, 22 says as much). In v 27, citing Ps 8:6, Paul appeals to the submission as a past fact: "For God 'has put everything under his feet.'" But then he has to modify this quotation, which perhaps was being used as a proof text at Corinth by those who rejoiced in the kingdom's fullness here and now, as they thought.

So Paul enters a double warning. He remarks on what is obvious with a moment's reflection, that God is not part of the present "reign of Christ" since it is God who is the one who does the subjecting. Paul needs to make room for a future "kingdom of God" as distinct from and subsequent to the present rule of Christ (v 24, which clearly separates the two kingdoms). Christ's present reign is by its nature an "in-between kingdom"—but not a millennial reign which some have discovered here, paralleling Rev 20:1–10—that is prepa-ratory to the ultimate divine reality of which v 28 speaks.

The other caution comes in v 28a, introduced by the words, "But when he has done this" or, with a variant trans-lation which is possible, "But when all things are subject to him [Christ]." Either way, Paul manifestly regards this sub-jection of "all things" to Christ as an event in the indetermi-nate future that, logically, has not yet taken place.

(ii) The present fact, however, is not in doubt. Christ has begun his reign now. Victory over malevolent powers is known in the experience of forgiveness of sins, as Paul has already linked that forgiveness to Christ's work in death and resurrection (15:4, 17). The enemies of God's people are therefore defeated in principle by Christ's resurrection tri-umph. Their final annihilation and removal from the scene, however, awaits a public judgment on them; and that sen-tence, for the apostle, belongs to the future, the "not yet" needed to complement and complete the "already" secured redemption won at Easter day. The kingdom of Christ is now; the final kingdom of God will be then.

It is in worship that the New Testament church pictures the present Lordship of Christ. There it focuses on the en-throned Lord, and it sees God's total rule over all evil forces as an accomplished fact. The songs of victory (heard in Phil 2:9–11; Eph 1:20–22; 4:8–10; 1 Pet 3:22; Rev 3:21; 5:1–14) remain rooted in history, and never move far from the scenes of historical redemption anchored to the cross of Good Fri-day. But their vision is elongated to reach into the future in order to bring it near. Thus they can speak of and celebrate Christ's future triumph as though it were a present reality— as indeed it is to the church at worship caught up to the heavenly world.

But the dangers of such triumphalism, if understood and celebrated without the counterbalancing reminder of the church's existence in the present evil age, are only too painfully obvious. Sin, mortality, and satanic powers are still alive and active in the world and the church. The future reign of God is not yet, however much we wish to see it and must work to promote its coming. It remains a hope to beckon us, and a challenge to inspire us. And in Christian worship which is celebratory in tone and based on a redemption that is already won for us the church greets the far-off divine event and seeks to order its life under the present leadership of its risen Lord. It is mindful, at the same time, that it has a future hope and so remains a pilgrim people who have not yet entered into the full and final inheritance that awaits them.

3. A recall and "representation" of what Christ did once for all in his Incarnation and death is at the heart of the Lord's Supper, as described in 1 Cor 11:23-26. At the center of the Christian memorial feast are the interpreting words spoken over the bread and the cup: "This is my body which is for you. Do this in remembrance of me. . . . This cup is the new covenant in my blood. Do this, as often as you drink it, in remembrance of me" (vv 24, 25, RSV). The "sacramental" significance of these words may be discussed later as we consider the nature of the Christian life for Paul in these letters. It is enough now to note that Christ's coming into the world is intimately bound up with his "sacrifice"; body and blood given for others are two metaphors shot through with ideas drawn from the Old Testament-Jewish world of sacrifice and offering, reminding us of the Passover ritual which is explicitly in Paul's mind in 1 Cor 5:7, 8:

Christ, our passover lamb, has been sacrificed. Let us, then, keep the festival . . . with the unleavened bread of sincerity and truth.

4. The mention of Christ in a typological fashion which sees him prefigured in the Old Testament rite (Exod 12) paves the way for a consideration of 1 Cor 10:1–13. This passage will be mentioned again when we discuss the church as the new Israel, when contrasts will be drawn between the Corinthians and the people of Israel passing through the Red Sea and the wilderness, and the application made to the Israel of the new covenant. In this connection Paul makes use of a tradition found among rabbinic commentators and in Philo that the rock from which the Jews drank followed the people (10:4). *Tosefta Sukkah* 3.11 gives the most dramatic version on this mobile rock. Based on an interpretation of Num 21:16–18, it was concluded that Miriam's well, shaped like a rock, kept pace with Israel's journeys over mountains and in valleys. Philo connects the moving rock with wisdom (*Leg. All.* 2.286). The latest commentator[1] plays down the link with Philo and prefers to see as Paul's main source the designation of Israel's God as the Rock (in Deut 32:4, 15, 18, 30, 31). As Yahweh was rejected by the wilderness generation (Deut 32:15, 18), so Christ's presence in the "spiritual" food and drink of the sacraments was abused at Corinth.

What is of interest is the way Paul openly connects this rock with Christ: "the rock was Christ" (v 4). The notion of Christ as in some unexplained way present before his birth as a human being and a member of Israel's community (Gal 4:4) is certainly arresting; and its use here is evidently intended to give a Christian flavor to the "eating and drinking" acts which are common to Israel in the desert and the church in the sacramental actions of baptism and the Lord's supper. Whether Paul held consciously to an understanding of Christ as possessing pretemporal existence, that is, he was alive in God before his coming to this world, is a matter that has divided recent students of Paul. Certainly 1 Cor 10:4 could be interpreted in this way, though it could equally be no more than a picturesque and forceful illustration to drive home Paul's point.

5. Other passages in the Corinthian correspondence are more explicit. If the issue is whether Paul believed that Christ was "preexistent" in the sense we have given it, 2 Cor 8:9 says clearly that the Incarnation did involve a change of existence. He who was with God became one with creation in order to elevate those who, though part of his creation, may come to share the life of God himself. That statement, we believe, would be fair comment on and summary of what Paul writes in more compelling terms:

> For you know the generosity of our Lord Jesus Christ who—for your sakes and though he was wealthy—became poor, so that you by that poverty might become wealthy.

We may pause to observe where Paul places the emphasis as he writes on the condescension of Christ's coming. "The grace of our Lord Jesus Christ" is the frontispiece of his declaration, as it becomes the first part of the apostolic benediction in 13:14. Whether this means simply, "You know how gracious the Lord Jesus Christ was," or has a deeper meaning, such as "You recall the event in grace which brought the Lord Jesus Christ into the world," is not certain. The divine title with "our" in 8:9 (and in 1 Cor 1:2) suggests that Paul is quoting a fixed liturgical formula, and is commenting on the stupendous miracle of God-becoming-human. Hence we may prefer the latter alternative if the verse is a preformed sentence borrowed by Paul. In support of the first option, however, which has "generosity" in the translation, is the relevance of that word to Paul's context. He is appealing for a generous response to the collection, and points to the highest example of generosity in the Incarnation.

In his being with God he was "rich," a term suggesting the desirability and honor that belonged to his status. It is parallel with Phil 2:6: "being in the form of God," which in turn seems to imply a condition or status that ranked him on the side of God over against the rest of creation, whether angelic or human. Col 1:15 expresses the same truth in terms of his being the "image of the unseen God," a designation drawn from the Wisdom literature (Wisd Sol 7), in which wisdom is described in highly personalized terms as enjoying intimate associations with the Most High (Prov 8; Sirach 24). Interestingly, James 2:1, which is an unlikely source in New Testament christology, speaks of Jesus Christ the Lord in exactly this way as one who shares and expresses the glory of God, as in 2 Cor 4:4-6 which repeats the imagery of Christ as the "image of God." *Eikon* (Paul's word in 4:4) means more than mirror or likeness, however; it carries the idea that Christ is the faithful representation of God's eternal nature since he shares in that nature. So it is a natural consequence for Paul to write that God's glory is to be seen in the face or person of Christ (4:6, akin to John 1:14, 18; Heb 1:1-3).

Form, image, glory: these are all picture terms for conveying the idea of a personal relationship that joined the preincarnate Christ with the Father. Paul's word here is "rich" which adds in the dimension of an estate to be highly valued and (maybe) retained at all costs.

"He did not consider equality with God as a prize to be exploited" (Phil 2:6) is one way to render the next phrase in the drama of the story of Christ. The Pauline text is a deep mystery, but at least it tells us that there was a decision to be made, and at some cost. Instead of viewing his prize of divine equality as an occasion for getting still more honor he chose to see it as a giving—of himself. This "decision" led directly to his becoming one with us in an act Paul in our verse calls "becoming poor." If we are correct in setting this dramatic condescension in the framework of the Incarnation, then poverty cannot be reduced to material lack (even though, at first glance, that is the theme of Paul's application to the Corinthians in discussing the collection for the saints). Christ became poor by accepting our human lot, what Paul elsewhere calls an emptying (kenosis, Phil 2:7) and becoming a slave, that is, a servant to obey his vocation in obedience and service for others. The ultimate cost is not left in doubt. He became obedient to death, and that death put him on a cross (Phil 2:8; see Heb 10:5-10 for similar conclusions).

Poverty and riches are the twin polarities of the purpose underlying what Paul is writing about. The believers for whose sake the Lord came to identify with them in their humanness and sin are the direct beneficiaries of all he did. They are raised to share in his life with God, and to enter with him into his glory (Rom 8:17).

This noble confession of faith centering on the major motifs in the saga of Christ has a practical purpose. It is intended to awaken the spirit of generous giving. But for all its incidental character its broad scope and amazing sweep of christological thought should not be missed. The picture Paul has and presents is of the heavenly Lord who laid aside his glory and oneness with God in order to make himself one with the poverty and wretchedness of the human condition. By this "downward" movement of his coming from God he intended to lift us to new heights of intimate fellowship with our creator and to share the relationship he also has enjoyed. Our destiny, Paul writes elsewhere (Rom 8:29), is to be conformed to the image of Christ as God's Son, in order that he might be the first-born in the family of God.

6. "He came from God" is the way 2 Cor 8:9 may be understood. But such a phrase hardly does justice to what 2 Cor 5:19 says:

In Christ God was reconciling the world to himself.

This enigmatic sentence may be taken in two or three different ways. The phrase "in Christ" may go with "God" to form a composite expression, thus God-in-Christ with the participle of the verb to follow. Or else "in Christ" refers to the means through which God reconciled the world (so Barrett). Yet another sense is supplied by attaching God in Christ to the verb in an imperfect or continuous tense, i.e., "God in Christ was reconciling the world to himself."

Paul's Greek, even if it is a quotation he uses, is less than precise; yet the sense required in the entire paragraph and the flow of the argument may point to the conclusion that Paul needs to show how God himself is personally involved. V 18 stresses how he acted through the agency of Christ (*dia Christou* means just that). Unless v 19 is a piece of tautology, repeating the same idea for the sake of emphasis, it needs to say something more than v 18. We interpret it as God's coming himself in Christ (*en Christo*) to our world. While the chief stress falls on divine reconciliation, Paul goes beyond the idea of agency (v 18) and mediation (mentioned in v 20: *hyper Christou*). He places at the center the affirmation of divine identification to underscore the personal presence of God who in Jesus Christ entered our time-bound order and made himself one with the human race he came to reconcile and restore.

> He sent no angel to our race,
> Of higher or of lower frame;
> But wore the robe of human form,
> And to our lost world came.

Paul's argument almost demands that the text in v 19 should mean something like this: in Christ God became one of our human family and identified himself with it both in its humanness and so in its sinfulness (5:21).

7. To place a capstone on Paul's expression of who Jesus

Christ was and is, the term *Lord* needs to be reckoned with. One of the fullest expositions of how Paul conceived of Christ's Lordship is in 1 Cor 8:5, 6 which we considered earlier. We now return to this passage with an inquiry as to how it "explains" the relation that Jesus Christ sustains to the various areas of Christian belief. In particular let us note how Paul relates Christ's title and office to God himself, the cosmos, and the church.

"One Lord" marks out the figure of Jesus as different from and opposed to the "many lords" (v 5) of contemporary hellenistic and oriental cults, and especially as opposed to the growing veneration of the Roman emperor as "lord" (Latin *dominus*). Serapis was a popular deity hailed as lord by followers in the cult that revered the god as a helper and savior.[2] Equally, with elements drawn from Egyptian religion, Isis was a familiar goddess in the Greece of Paul's day. The healer Asclepius commanded a wide following and devotion at Corinth where recent excavations have brought the ruins of an Asclepion (a complex of buildings devoted to the worship of the god) to light and he was known as "lord." Soon the Roman emperor would make a bold claim that he or his genius was worthy of worship and, as Suetonius was later to report of Domitian (in the nineties of the era), would have temples built to revere him as "our lord and god" (*dominus et deus*).

For Paul the monotheistic Jew, all this would have been abhorrent, however much he might sympathize with the human aspirations for guidance, healing, and authority these cults were designed to meet. Yet he is forthright in claiming that Jesus Christ, a figure in recent history, who lived and died in Palestine within living memory, could only be regarded as "Lord" in the truest sense of that title. Moreover, Jesus stood over against human beings (though one with the rest of creation by choice and design, as we just observed) and on the side of God. "Lord" representing the title accorded to Israel's covenant God in the Greek Bible is appropriated as the suitable honorific name of the one whom God highly exalted and installed as *Kyrios* (Phil 2:9-11).

The cosmic background to the title "Lord" is also to be seen in 1 Cor 8:6. The one Lord, Jesus Christ is hailed as the one "through whom all things came to be." This reference is tantalizingly obscure since it has no verb, and we are compelled to insert "came to be" to complete the sense. The passage is part of a hymnic or poetic tribute to the persons in the Christian godhead. "One Lord" is, as we saw, a confession of a single Lordship in a polytheistic society of competing divinities. "All things" refers to cosmic power, as in the parallel hymnic acclamation of Col 1:15-20; and Paul associates the creation of the universe, believed to be linked with cosmic and astral powers, with the preexisting Christ who was the divinely appointed agent by whom God made the world. John 1:3 and Heb 1:2 are closely parallel and relate the action of God in the beginning with the activity of the Logos-Wisdom figures that the early Christians saw to be an allusion to the cosmic Lord known to them as Jesus Christ.

*Kyrios*, "Lord," is a title that may have arisen in early Christian circles as a result of biblical exegesis in Old Testament passages such as 2 Cor 3:15-18 or, perhaps more probably, as a consequence of Christians' setting Jesus at the center of their worship and calling on his name in a manner akin to the way Jews were said to identify themselves as Yahweh's devotees. It cannot be accidental, then, that this is how Paul designates the believing community in southern Greece at the head of 1 Cor. He greets the church of God at Corinth "with all those who in every place call on the name of our Lord Jesus Christ, both their Lord and ours" (1 Cor 1:2).

The precise expression "to call on the name of" the deity is both an act of confession (as in Rom 10:12-14) and an affirmation of belonging to the one whose name is thereby invoked. The phrase denotes—in the Old Testament—allegiance to Yahweh as Israel's covenant God (e.g., Gen 21:33 used of Abraham, the father of the faithful). In the New Testament generally and even in 1 Cor 1:2 in particular it is a sign and badge of belonging to the God of the promise made to Abraham which was fulfilled in Christ (2 Cor 1:20) and so, by transference, of belonging to Christ as Lord who is ranked as God. It is a natural corollary for Paul to make this shift from Yahweh to Christ in 2 Cor 3:17:

> "The Lord" [in the passage cited from Exod 34:34 which speaks of Moses' turning to God] represents the Spirit; and wherever the Spirit of the Lord is, there is freedom.

Yet "Lord" is more than a title for understanding the Old Testament and a label to denote one's belonging to a new master; it is intensely practical and down-to-earth. Kyrios stands for the authority to which men and women are accountable and it is in the light of that responsibility they have to view their decisions and actions. This application comes out clearly in 1 Cor 6:12–19 and 7:17–24.

The first passage has to do with Christian morality which Paul interprets in the light of the use of the body. The details may be given in a later discussion; here we are content simply to draw attention to 6:17: "But he who is united to the Lord becomes one spirit with him."

The apostle is obviously making a play—although in a serious vein—with the word "united." The erring Corinthians saw no harm or inconsistency in becoming united with prostitutes at the local brothel, on the mistaken assumption no doubt that once their spirits were "saved," they could indulge their bodily appetites and libido without restraint or conscience. Paul retorts that a union of this kind is unthinkable for a professed Christian, whose true union is with the Lord as part of the nuptial bond (Gen 2:24; see 2 Cor 11:2) connecting Christ and his spouse. So the imperative is clear: shun immoral relations that destroy the union between the Lord and his people (6:18). Owning him as Lord has a direct bearing on one's sexual and social conduct, and no fancy theologizing to do with being raised with Christ and so beyond the reach of high moral claims can ever excuse a Christian who allows his or her passions to be dominant. "All is permitted" (6:12) was the Corinthian slogan, which reappears in our day as "everything goes; if it feels good, do it." Paul's thunderous comment and corrective is quickly added: "But I will not be brought under the power of anything." How can he when he has professed Christ as Lord, as the sole authority and ruling power in his life?

The second passage sets the same idea in the context of the social problems occasioned by slavery (1 Cor 7:17–24). Slavery was a commonplace part of the Greco-Roman society in which the church was born. Paul raised no standard of revolt against this inhuman institution. We may ask why he did not—and find part of the answer in his letter to Philemon where "emancipation" (but not by a slaves' uprising, which would have disastrous results for all concerned as Spartacus's rebellion proved) trembles on his lips (in v 16). He adds a new dimension, hitherto unrecognized—taking the truant slave Onesimus back "no longer as a slave but more than a slave, as a dear brother, especially to me but how much to you, both in the flesh and in the Lord."

The last phrase from Philem 16 provides a clue to understanding the passage in 1 Cor 7. There were opportunities for a slave to find freedom, chiefly by the payment of a sum of money deposited in a temple and transferred to the slave's owner, as the hundreds of names, inscribed in gratitude, on the walls of Apollo's shrine at Delphi testify. Paul encourages this procedure (7:21), but then moves from the relationship "in the flesh," i.e., as a human being in society, to the relationship "in the Lord" which comes in the reminder that all his readers, whether slaves or free persons, are under the vow of obedience and loyalty to a higher power, namely Christ the Lord. The fact that in Greek one word (kyrios) may mean both an owner of slaves and the heavenly Lord Jesus facilitated this transition of thought. All the Corinthians in their society—whether slave master, free people, or slaves—are "bought at a price" (7:23). The same verse adds a new perspective, which may be called "living under Christ's Lordship," and the effect on this moral mandate is to be seen in the so-called Station Codes of Eph 6:5–9 and Col 3:22–4:1 (cf. 1 Pet 2:18–21).

One final reference to the Lordship of Christ claims our attention. The way that the Lord's power was exercised, both as seen in the church's Lord and then by extension in the lives of his apostolic representatives, was a topic of burning concern in the last four chapters of 2 Corinthians, the so-called "Letter of Conflict." The sense turns on what kind of Lordship Christ was known to have commanded, and so on the question of how his earthly agents model their styles of authority.

Paul's answer to both questions is one and the same. The power of Christ was held in restraint and he acted in lowliness and meekness (2 Cor 10:1). He died in weakness on the cross, and at the resurrection the authority he assumed still bore the mark of humility and grace (2 Cor 13:4). So his followers and agents are called to be primarily his servants (2 Cor 4:5), treading in the path of the servant Messiah whose title to Lordship is most evident in a continuing ministry of service and love. See 2 Cor 13:10 where Paul, in direct contrast to those who came as emissaries to Corinth and adopted a haughty disposition and ruled over the congregation with unfeeling arrogance (2 Cor 11:19), sets out the true ministry of the apostles of the Lord:

*The Grace and Glory of Our Lord Jesus Christ*

When I am present I might not have to act harshly in accordance with the authority which the Lord has given me, the authority for building you up, not tearing you down.

Equally impressive is the self-confession of an apostolic lifestyle in 2 Cor 1:24:

This does not mean that we are ruling over your faith, but we are working with you for your joy.

Both pieces of Pauline pastoralia show how clearly he understood his mission and how fully he had grasped the Lordship of the Christ who was among his disciples as one who serves (Luke 22:27).

# 5    THE GOSPEL, THE SPIRIT, AND
##      THE CONGREGATION

Paul's mission preaching at Corinth is spelled out in two places. The evidence of Acts 18:1–18 gives some interesting pointers to the way Luke describes Paul's ministry; and there is the no less informative statement in 1 Cor chs 1 and 2.

Acts 18 regards Paul's initial evangelism as one of "arguing" and "persuading" (18:4, 13). When Silas and Timothy came from Macedonia, no doubt bearing the gifts of the Philippians (2 Cor 11:9; Phil 4:15–18), Paul was released from some financial constraints which required him to do manual work as a tentmaker, a practice he had adopted from his stay in Thessalonica (1 Thess 2:9; 2 Thess 3:9; cf. Acts 20:34). He began, we are told, to devote himself wholeheartedly to the ministry of preaching (Acts 18:5) as he bore witness to the Jews that Jesus was the fulfillment of Israel's messianic hopes.

Some success attended these efforts, but there was also opposition and discouragement. The verdict of Gallio's tribunal settled the first issue, thereby allowing Paul to continue his pastoral work for some considerable time (Acts 18:18). The vision he received of the heavenly Lord who reassured him of both divine protection and a reward for his labors prompted him to continue his endeavors, "teaching the word of God among them" (Acts 18:11).

So far the narrative in Acts is circumstantial and reportorial. We need to go behind the scenes to learn from the Corinthian letters something of the apostle's frame of mind and disposition as he came to Corinth from the almost total rejection he had experienced at Athens (Acts 17:32-34).

At 1 Cor 1:18 Paul is led into a discussion by the thought that if the preacher uses words of eloquent wisdom the inevitable result is that the cross of Christ is rendered ineffective. The content of that message is then powerfully expounded and its effect on those who come within earshot of it is clearly shown (vv 18-25). Three types of reaction are a Christian response, a Jewish refusal, and a Greek rejection:

## Christ the power of God

(a) To those "who are being saved" (a present tense) the cross represents the epitome of divine power, leading to salvation (Rom 1:16). The association of power with the humiliation and ignominy of death on a Roman gibbet—a death reserved for the most degraded and despised in Roman society and regarded with universal horror as the "most cruel and shocking of all punishments" (Cicero)—would seem very surprising. At first sight the link of power and the cross is certainly a paradox (see 2 Cor 13:4), since the display of force and a submission to a shameful death in which the victim is most helpless and unable to move himself hold together mutually contradictory ideas.

But Paul goes on to explain that in the very weakness of God, who in Christ suffered defeat at the hands of wicked men, divine wisdom is revealed and the heart of God is made known (1 Cor 1:25). What could never be grasped by human inquiry or discovery stands open to full view at the cross, as the Spirit illumines the mind to appreciate and accept that in this act in history much more than the death of the man Jesus of Nazareth is involved. "In Christ God was reconciling the world to himself" (2 Cor 5:19) and in that mysterious event the sins of the world are carried away and the new age of divine salvation is introduced. Those who have found in Christ crucified the secret of life's purpose and God's plan, decreed from of old (1 Cor 2:7-10), realize that it is God's initiative and power that have led them to this blessedness; and so they give him their thanks for undeserved mercies shown to sinners who are now set on the road to salvation (1 Cor 1:21, 31; 2 Cor 9:15).

(b) "But they have not all heeded the gospel" (Rom 10:16). The proclamation of the cross, of Christ crucified for our sins (1 Cor 15:3) and so the ground of our hope of eschatological salvation in the new world of God's righteous rule (2 Cor 5:21), then as now, divides people into the stark categories of those who respond and those who reject.

The Jewish hearers, with their insistent demand for "signs"—a feature seen in the ministry of Jesus from its beginning (Matt 4:1-11; Luke 4:1-13) to its close (Mark 15:32), but at its most dramatic in the episode of Mark 8:11-13—refuse to believe that a crucified man can be their Messiah. Deut 21:23 proves that he must be under a divine curse. How can Messiah, a title of undisputed favor and honor, be identified with one who died "on a tree," that is, as an outcast from Israel's covenant community and under the ban of excommunication? It is small wonder that the Jews drew the conclusion that Paul's message was impossible to believe.

Paul concludes that, seen solely in the light of the Deuteronomic verse, the cross is and remains a "scandal," a roadblock on the way to faith. But, as we learn from his wrestling with the same problem, light is given in two ways:

the crucified Jesus suffered and died, not for his own crimes but he died for others. So Deut 21:23 proves exactly what the Jewish debaters were denying: He became a curse for us (Gal 3:13, which goes on to quote the OT proof-text). Second, the cross has to be seen in the light of the resurrection which, for Paul ever since his thinking was reoriented on the Damascus road, reversed the judgment of Good Friday and vindicated both the faithful ministry of Jesus and God's strength-in-weakness (2 Cor 13:4). Paul's rejoinder, when faced with the paradox of the cross, is to proclaim boldly: He died an accursed death, but he assumed our curse (2 Cor 5:21). He died our death, but God brought him out of defeat and shame to the glory of Easter which is his glory (1 Cor 15:42–45).

(c) The Greeks found the cross to be a huge joke (1 Cor 1:23). It contradicted their cherished notions of divine wisdom; indeed, it taught the precise opposite of their axiom that the gods cannot and do not suffer mortal pain. The Greek divinities inhabited a lotus-land far removed from human misery. They remained aloof and were untouched by human misery. A good illustration comes in Aristophanes' play, *The Frogs* (lines 632–34). The scene is set in the underworld of Hades where two travelers are each claiming to be divine. A simple test is devised to sort out the true from the false claimant, who is the god and who is his slave:

> You should flog him well,
> For if he is god he won't feel it.
> Whichever of the two you first see
> Flinching or crying out—he's not the god.

The Christian answer lies in a God who entered our human life at every level, and tasted death at its bitterest. This is divine wisdom in a mystery, and shows that "the foolishness of God is wiser than men" (1:25).

The counterpart to the Jews' insistence on credentials (1:22) was the Greeks' love of oratory and impressive public speaking. To them the acme of learning was the presentation of a well-ordered and persuasively uttered discourse on some lofty (and preferably novel) theme (Acts 17:21).

It is not therefore to be wondered at that Paul's preaching in Athens should be dismissed as the weird pronouncement of a babbler (Acts 17:18-20). And Paul possibly felt that little good had been accomplished at Athens when he moved on to Corinth. But it would be too much to infer that he wrote 1 Cor 2:1-5 in retrospect of having "failed" at Athens and that he resolved after that experience to abandon completely the more philosophical approach to preaching the good news.

More likely, when faced with the challenges of Corinthian culture and the needs that were evident in such a place, he came to see with particular intensity that his ministry was to offer a straightforward presentation of the cross (2:2). He would present a message decked out with no human embellishments (2:1) and conveyed with no reliance on rhetorical persuasion (2:4).

Indeed, his bearing and public proclamation were just the opposite of the qualities that marked out the accomplished Greek orator and debater. He came to Corinth "in weakness and in much fear and trembling" (2:3). He placed his sole reliance on the Spirit to provide both the proof and the power to drive home the message (2:4). His objective is clearly stated: "that your faith might not rest in human wisdom but in the divine power" the Spirit affords (2:5).

This is a most revealing section, and may be said to be the first comment from Paul's pen on an issue that runs through the correspondence with Corinth. The charge that his person and his speech were beneath contempt would surface again in 2 Corinthians (10:10). And Paul would be forced on

to the defensive from the emissaries who came with allegations that he was no rhetorically trained or gifted speaker,
whatever his skills as a letter-writer at a safe distance may have
been (2 Cor 10:1-2, 9). Paul does not deny the accusation,
which is cited in 10:10; and at 11:6 he concedes the point that
he is unskilled in public speaking. But he has already made it
plain that his "simple" preaching style was one he had chosen
to cultivate for theological reasons, namely that only in this
way could the true nature of the gospel be honored and the
Corinthians would be led to see that their faith was the gift
of the Holy Spirit (1 Cor 12:3) and not the result of human
persuasiveness such as popular speakers in hellenistic society
exploited (2 Cor 2:17).

It is no contradiction of the disavowal of Paul to resort to
rhetorical devices when he proceeds to claim the gift of wisdom (1 Cor 2:6). The same gift is traced to the Spirit's activity
(1 Cor 12:8), so there cannot be anything pejorative about
that claim: "among the mature (Gr. teleioi, a play on the word
which evidently was part of the Corinthians' proud boast, "to
be perfect"; but Paul dismisses them as mere babes, 1 Cor
3:1-4; 13:11; 14:20) we do impart wisdom. . . . We impart a
secret and hidden wisdom of God."

The term "wisdom" needs a careful definition. Paul has
been at pains to show that the apostolic preaching of the cross
does not look to any human philosophy or man-devised argument for its persuasiveness and appeal. Reliance on such a
prop, he avers, is foredoomed to failure (1 Cor 1:21). The
"wisdom of this age" (2:6) is, above all, fleeting, and vain. This
is the conclusion he draws from the assurance that his message is based on God's truth and announced in dependence
on the Holy Spirit (2:4).

But there is a wisdom that is appropriate; it is based on
divine revelation, not human ingenuity (2:6), and it is commu-
nicated to believing men and women by the Spirit (2:10-12).
Wisdom is the gift of God; it leads to the true knowledge of

God, not speculation or theory; and it is the mark of the person who seeks to walk in God's way and obey his voice. From his Jewish teachers Paul had learned this lesson well, and it is boldly brought over into the full light of Christ who is the wisdom of God incarnate in human form (1 Cor 1:24).

"Wisdom" (*sophia*) plays a key role in the discussion of chapters 1–3 where the term is found sixteen times, while "the wise person" (*sophos*) recurs ten times in these chapters. C. K. Barrett[1] helpfully distinguishes four categories of the word's use.

As a "bad" term it represents the Greek sophist with his eloquence and prowess in debate, and it shades off into an arrogance that has no room for the cross (1:22, 2:6). On the "good" side it can describe the gift of eloquence as a Christian virtue (12:8, this is Barrett's classification of a nontechnical sense, which may be questioned), and it shines in its truest Pauline sense when it means an understanding of God's saving plan, as clearly in 1:24, 30; 2:6. In this last named category "wisdom" is the gift that comes alone from God who takes the initiative (2:10) and bestows the illumination of the Spirit (2:12) intended to make "us wise for salvation through faith in Christ Jesus" (2 Tim 3:15). This is elsewhere equivalent to the gift(s) of the Holy Spirit (2:14) to enable men and women to cry, "Jesus is Lord" (12:3) and to be baptized into the one body in the church's fellowship (12:13).

Since this understanding of the way the single term "wisdom" is used in its various connotations is so important for Paul, and indeed forms the basis for his evangelistic preaching, a review is in order (based on 1 Cor 2:6–16):

The bankruptcy of human wisdom, uninspired and uninformed by divine revelation, is seen most clearly in the way Christ was rejected and killed on the cross (2:8). The cross that men prepared for the Lord of glory became, for Paul, the supreme example and illustration of human perversity, opposition, and rejection. Yet to see the events of history on the surface did not go far enough. One must penetrate to the "hidden agenda" behind Good Friday. Beneath the evil designs of the Jewish leaders in the Sanhedrin and the callousness of the Roman authorities who carried out the sentence of death at Calvary stood the satanic agencies of evil spirit powers, surnamed "the rulers of this age" (2:8).

Paul will later in this correspondence revert to the theme of opposition from this quarter. In 2 Corinthians 4:4 he accounts for the strange blindness that afflicts unbelievers by reference to "the god of this age," an allusion to Satan the adversary of God and humankind. It was Satan's minions who conspired to do away with the Lord of glory, only to be startled to discover that what they plotted, planned, and executed led to their own undoing. A similar scenario, however strange it may seem to the modern interpreter, underlies another Pauline dramatic sidelight on the events of Good Friday (Col 2:15):

> He disarmed the principalities and powers and made a public example of them, triumphing over them in it, i.e., the cross. (RSV, marg.)

The underpinning of this amazing statement is worth investigating, with a brief rehearsal of what seems to be the rationale involved.

### The risen Lord

Paul's proclamation of the cross at Corinth was closely linked with the resurrection. This can be seen from the way he writes in 2 Cor 4:14. God is known as the one who "raised up Jesus" (from death). See too, 2 Cor 1:9 which Paul writes as a general description of God "who raises the dead"—a piece of liturgical praise, borrowed from the synagogue worship. For him, however, the event of resurrection in the case of

Jesus was invested with a tremendous significance, best seen in 2 Cor 5:17. With the coming and triumph of Christ over death a new world has been born, a new eschatological epoch is here. The ringing declaration of 1 Cor 15:20, "Christ has been raised from the dead," repeats that assurance.

But all Christian truth is vulnerable to misinterpretation and wrongful understanding. Heresy has been defined as truth carried to unwarranted limits, and thus exaggerated out of all proportion. So it was at Corinth. The believers there were led to see the present glory of the risen Lord as the all-consuming reality (the title "Lord of glory" in 1 Cor 2:8 may be the Corinthians' own ascription to Jesus). For them the existence of Christ covered a two-stage period: Jesus came into this world, and then he was promoted to a glorious state. At their baptism (as we saw) they came to share that glory, and to regard themselves as fully raised with Christ as men and women of the Spirit (see 1 Cor 2:15; if that too was a Corinthian slogan, it shows the practical effect of such a belief).

Paul was driven to oppose this understanding with a three-step movement, in which Christ's threefold status corresponds to Christian existence and experience. As we set down this response, it should be clear that we are ready to see how the saving message bears upon the teaching concerning the church in these letters.

(i) Christ died and was raised (1 Cor 15:20a). Here, in a pregnant sentence, Paul and his disputants are agreed, though the apostle found it needful to add the qualifier: "[Christ] is the first fruits of those who have died" (15:20b). He does so to ward off any suggestion that Christian resurrection has already taken place in baptism and that death can be avoided as a gateway to a future resurrection. This one reminder is really the key to unlock the main problem faced in 1 Cor 15.

(ii) Christ's present rule is a reality (as all concur) but only Paul emphasizes that it is a contested rule and is still

*The Gospel, the Spirit, and the Congregation*

incomplete. The old order still remains, with its sad signs of sickness, weakness, and above all death (1 Cor 15:26, 54–57). Hence Corinthian believers, though "raised" in baptism, continue to die (1 Cor 11:30); Paul is the ailing apostle who receives no physical cure (2 Cor 12:9, 10); and Satan is still at work in the world (2 Cor 4:4) and in opposing the church (1 Cor 5:5; 2 Cor 2:11; 11:14, 15; 12:7). The church lives in the "in-between" period which is the overlap of the epochs (1 Cor 10:11). It is caught in the tension of being part of fallen creation with its inherent weakness and proneness to sin (1 Cor 5:1–13; 10:1–13; 2 Cor 12:21) and its mortality in this age (1 Cor 7:31; 2 Cor 5:1–5), and being a present shrine of the Spirit (1 Cor 3:16–17) who is the pledge of future expectation (2 Cor 5:5) of new life.

(iii) Christ's future lies beyond the Parousia, Paul is confident (1 Cor 15:23–28). In the same way the believer's hope is set in the future triumph when the Spirit's guarantee (2 Cor 1:22) will be honored and God's ultimate reign will be achieved (1 Cor 15:28). The twin sacraments of baptism (1 Cor 10:1–13) and the Lord's supper (1 Cor 11:23–34) point forward to this time since both have a built-in eschatological dimension that prevents them from being taken as tokens of security in this age. This eschatological proviso also demands that believers look beyond the "symbol" of water, bread, and cup to that which they represent, actualize, and promise: The presence of the Lord who both came once into history, is coming to meet his people as they obey his commands, and will come at the end time. The ethical insistence on obedience and a lively faith is a safeguard lest the sacraments should be treated as magic or superstition—or, perhaps even worse, as a substitute for "faith working by love" (see Gal 5:6). The day of Christ will be an occasion of moral accountability when the church members will be called to a reckoning (1 Cor 4:5; 2 Cor 5:10); and no religious observance, however well regarded, will compensate for a failure to cultivate a high moral tone in Christian behavior or to practice a true community that cares for the poor and despised (1 Cor 11:20-34). "Discerning the body" (11:29, RSV) is best understood as treating one's underprivileged fellowbeliever in a way that befits the spirit of genuine *koinonia* (1 Cor 12:22-26).

### The shrine of the Spirit

Just as Paul links intimately the cross and the resurrection of Jesus as two sides of the same coin in order to bid his readers see the continuing power of the cross as being in no way swallowed up by the risen glory of Christ, so he introduces the work of the Holy Spirit in the church under a double aspect. The church is both a community indwelt and sanctified by the Spirit and a company of frail, erring men and women who need constantly to be watchful (1 Cor 16:13), to take heed to their profession (1 Cor 10:12), and to "perfect [their] holiness in the fear of God" (2 Cor 7:1). Above all, they are put on their mettle in regard to the call to true community life that does not allow pietistic individualism to make them uncaring, or to indulge their spirituality in the more exotic and demonstrable gifts of the Spirit that deny the very essence of the saving message that has brought the church into being.

These are the chief issues that concern us as we seek now to relate Paul's gospel at Corinth to its down-to-earth context in the life of Christians in community. Four images of the church dominate the scene.

The church is a *building* (1 Cor 3:9) in which Paul is the craftsman (1 Cor 3:10) though the foundation is Christ himself (1 Cor 3:11); and it is a *bride* of Christ with Paul's role that of the groomsman conducting the spouse to her husband (2 Cor 11:2, 3; cf. John 3:29). A variation on this latter theme is the church as family under the parenthood of God (2 Cor 6:18) who has both sons and daughters. The last word is significantly added to the OT reference in 2 Sam 7:14 (cf. Hos 1:10; Isa 43:6). Paul often regards himself in these epistles as the earthly parent of the Corinthians (1 Cor 4:14, 15; 2 Cor 6:13; 12:14). The third image picks up the theme of the church's role as a serving people (1 Cor 12:1–11) by utilizing the metaphor of the *body* (12:12–13). We must examine this third image in some detail. But it is the fourth way in which the church is depicted that looks to be most distinctive in the Corinthian writing. The church as a *temple of God* (1 Cor 3:16, 17; 6:19, 20; 2 Cor 6:14–7:1) paves the way for the relevance Paul must bring out as he shows how the church is called into being as a holy people of God.

(i) *The church as a holy people.* Paul's pastoral theology, with its strategic approach, is very clear at the outset of his Corinthian correspondence. The first letter will soon have to address serious moral issues and expose the woeful misunderstanding of what the Christians' vocation should be. But Paul opens with a note of greeting that sees the church as it was intended to be rather than what it actually was.

> To the church of God in Corinth, to those sanctified in Christ Jesus and called to be holy. . . . (1 Cor 1:2)

The link terms are "sanctified" and "called to be holy," and the common factor that unites them is the work of the Holy Spirit who is the author of new life (12:11) and the divine agent to ensure that the church is a true shrine for the worship of the holy God of Israel (see 1 Cor 6:19, 20).

The first readers must have been stabbed awake by these words when they were read out in public assembly. If the account in 1 Cor 6:9–11 is anywhere near the truth—and Paul would hardly have insulted and alienated his people by such a fearful tale of gross immorality if he intended to win them over to his side—the moral state in which the readers lived prior to their becoming Christians stood in direct contrast. To be a devotee of pagan idols (1 Cor 12:2) was bad in all conscience—from the Old Testament-Judaic angle, which is Paul's viewpoint. To be charged with all manner of pernicious and antisocial behavior would be a sad reminder. Yet against such a backcloth of some of them, the grace of God shines more luminously. Now—in Christ and by the sanctifying Spirit—they have been washed clean, made holy, and set in right relationship with God. That was God's intention for his people; and Paul does well to remind them at the outset that, on God's side, all provision for human restoration has been made. This ideal must challenge their present state, and alert them to what should be their true calling as the holy people of God in continuity with ancient Israel, a people also called to be "holy to Yahweh," as the "saints of God."

To be numbered among "the saints" on its biblical background implies two ideas. There is the thought of separation from all that is evil and morally offensive to God; but given with equal emphasis is the idea that God's holy people are dedicated to his service and truly belong to him as his possession. Paul will illustrate the tension between what the Corinthians are in Christ, as sharers in the new eschatological age (2 Cor 5:17), and what is to be their life in this present wicked world. He employs Old Testament imagery for this purpose to set forth the "eschatological tension" between God's ideal and the need for believers to rise to their high destiny.

## (a) 1 Corinthians 5:6–8

A reading of 5:1–5 is really mandatory to set the scene. Paul can hardly credit it, but reports have confirmed that the church has lost all sense of moral responsibility and is actually condoning a glaring case of incest. Indeed, the matter is aggravated not only by the failure to deal with the offender, but by the church's attitude of continued arrogance (5:2). This may imply that what to Paul should have been an occasion of discipline had been treated as a matter of some self-congratulation; and would point to the idea that some Corinthians had accepted a gnosticizing teaching which devalued bodily "sins" as immaterial once the spirit had been saved. At all events, Paul knows what must be done. This loose morality—for whatever reason it may claim to be excused—must be strongly rejected (5:2b).

To drive home his ethical call Paul uses the illustrative procedures of Passover. Before the days of the feast a ceremony was—and still is in the homes of pious Jews—performed to search out and destroy all traces of yeast or any kind of fermenting material. In old editions of the Passover service-book a picture of an old man with a candle is often placed as a frontispiece. This represents God who will search Jerusalem with lamps (Zeph 1:12), and is thereby encouraging Jewish housewives to do the same! At the close of the search, on the eve of Passover, a solemn declaration by the housewife is made that if any leaven has been inadvertently overlooked in the kitchen or house, it is pronounced null and void.

Leaven is a symbol of evil, suggesting to the rabbis that the rising of the dough is an apt picture of the swelling of pride. The Jews, at Passover, must be reminded that they were a poor and servile people when the Lord redeemed them from Egypt (Deut 7:6-11; 26:5-9). Against such a background the Corinthians are called to (i) clear out every trace of moral evil (5:7) by dealing with the presence of arrogant sin in their midst (5:13); (ii) recall that they are the new Israel of God, summoned to be a holy people to the Lord and redeemed by the Paschal Lamb himself, who is typified in the lambs of Exod 12:3-7; and (iii) celebrate their new life as a festival of joy and gladness with a recall that they should become what they are: "that you may be a new batch without yeast—as you really are" (5:7). This is one of the clearest evidences of Paul's fundamental position in regard to ethical questions. He calls believers to act out their new status in Christ, to become what they in fact are.

### (b) 1 Corinthians 10:1-13

The church is the heir to Old Testament promises—and warnings. This salutary reflection on the need to live in the light of the believer's calling prompted Paul to deal with a prevailing mood at Corinth. The pith of his admonition is that outward profession, expressed in a confidence that once baptism had been administered all was well, is "no safeguard for a careless life which takes liberties with itself" (Moffatt).[2] This is the reminder in 1 Corinthians 10. He recalls how the Old Testament people of God had their special "moments of revelation" when God came uniquely near. They enjoyed their "sacraments" as they were "baptized into Moses" (10:2) and were sustained by the living-giving water out of the rock (10:4). But, as they turned aside to idolatry, and became apostate from the true God, they quickly met a sorry fate (10:5-10).

Paul takes these incidents—five in number, in Num 11:4-6; Exod 32:6; Num 25:1-9; 21:4-9; 16—and invests them with a significance for the church to which he is writing. The call is one of self-examination (10:12) and it rebukes all presumption and blind trust in religious ceremonial or any "once for all" status that makes the believers insensitive to the moral standards set by the gospel and demanded of God's church in every age.

The punch line is in 10:14: "Therefore, my dear friends, flee from idolatry." Put in another way, Paul is calling on the church to respect its dignity as God's ransomed community and to live in the light in its professed vocation as a holy people.

### (c) 2 Cor 6:14–7:1

The critical questions of how this passage fits into the flow of Paul's thought and the presence of unusual language and idioms should not obscure the deeper issue of how it brings to light the true nature of the church. If we read, in swift succession, 6:11–13 and 7:2–4 we are bound to think that the intervening verses are an interlude as a digression or even an insertion into the text. But it would be a hasty judgment to conclude that 6:14–7:1 is out of place in the context.

Paul is dealing with a refractory group in the church that is opposed to him and his gospel. He uses the appeal to the gospel (in 5:20) to summon them to be reconciled to God—by coming back to his cause and receiving him as their true apostle (6:13). Now he offers an exposition on the church as a neo-levitical community patterned on Lev chaps 17–26 to drive home both the real nature of the church as the temple of the Lord, consecrated for holy worship and the folly of the readers' ranging themselves on the side of the world, called unbelieving and set under the power of Satan (Belial) or idols. By a single stroke, using a series of Old Testament quotations and allusions (six in number), he establishes the holy destiny of the church at Corinth. So doing, he summons the disobedient members to respect their calling and leave the world's side in order to attach themselves resolutely to his gospel and apostleship. It is another way of saying to them, "We urge you not to receive God's grace in vain" (6:1), which is what they would be doing if they remained recalcitrant and failed to recognize their life as God's sanctified church.

(ii) *The church as a worshiping, serving, witnessing community.* Our attention is now directed to 1 Cor chs 12–15 which are taken up with one central theme. At first sight the discussion centers on "spiritual gifts" (12:1) but, as we get into these chapters, it becomes clear that the organizing topic that pulls into its orbit several Corinthian and Pauline concerns is rather the nature of the church and its place in God's plan of salvation in this age. This is why chapter 15 is an integral part of the entire section, and really holds the key to the earlier chapters.

In summary, the main problem at Corinth was a theological one, and was focused on a denial of a future for the church (1 Cor 15:12). As we noted, a false notion of baptismal resurrection (1 Cor 4:8) gave some in the church the idea that, already raised with Christ, they had entered upon a heavenly existence now with a type of ecstatic worship that matched their celestial status. The question of Paul's authority was at risk as well, and it seems that some women prophetesses (1 Cor 14:34–38) had stepped out of line by introducing this teaching which thrust the cross into the background and maximized the practical implication of the resurrection here and now. A denial of a future resurrection and a climax to history led Paul into one of his most complete expositions on the resurrection hope.

The chief thrust of chapter 15 is to oppose those who held to four ideas simultaneously: (1) there is no resurrection in the future (they alleged) because it has already occurred in baptism (misunderstanding Rom 6:1–6); (2) there is no need to anticipate the future because they believed they had total salvation without remainder here and now. A popular version of this mistake shows that the error is still with us. Recently a slogan was coined, "Let's stop singing 'In the Sweet Bye-and-Bye,' and start celebrating about the fantastic Now-and-Now." (3) "How are the dead raised?" (v 35a) challenges the whole idea of resurrection after death; and (4) "with what kind of body do they come?" (v 35b) casts doubt on the notion of personal and bodily survival.

Paul's argument is designed to meet each of these four points. Building on the creedal affirmations (15:3–11) he goes on to assert: death must precede resurrection as in the case of Jesus himself; the hope of the resurrection lies in the future, when he comes (v 23); Christ's resurrection after he died proves that resurrection is God's plan for his people; and at the Parousia there will be a transformation of both the departed and the living to account for a new bodily resurrection (vv 44, 50-57).

With this hermeneutical key we can now approach chapters 12-14 under some customary headings.

### (a) The Christian's Lord and Service

Paul is led into this theme as he gives answers to queries brought by the Corinthians themselves. The initial theme is "spiritual gifts" (as in 14:1) within the setting of public worship, as is evident from 11:2-16, 17-34. By comparison he uses other phrases to denote private or family worship (14:4, 35) whereas his main interest is what goes on in a church context (see 12:27; 14:5, 19, 26, 33, 35). Certain practices, e.g., speaking in tongues, are permitted freely in a personal way, but in a church service other factors need to be reckoned with, such as the need to supply interpretation (14:5, 27, 28), the importance of building up the whole church (14:4, 31) and the effect on outsiders (14:23-25).

In 12:1-3 Paul states the test of all "gifts of the Spirit," thereby announcing the axiom that the church lives by confessing Christ as Lord. Not all religious experience is genuinely Christian; in fact, some types are frankly pagan (12:2) and other manifestations (as in v 3) are shown to be sub-Christian by using language that is either inadequate ("Jesus is anathema," in the sense of Gal 3:13) or blasphemous ("Jesus is cursed," a verdict that became a sign of the disavowal of one's faith, as in the choice presented to Polycarp in the early second century). Authentic Christian experience stands under the Lordship of Christ (Rom 10:9, 10) and is the work of the Holy Spirit (John 15:26), with the reminder that it is the Spirit's ministry to bind together the historical Jesus and the Christ of faith so closely that both aspects are mutually illuminating and necessary.

The same Spirit, having imparted the gift of the saving confession ("Jesus is Lord"), proceeds to enable all Christians, baptized into one body (12:12, 13), to perform a variety of tasks in a section where v 4 is matched by v 11. Three principles are made visible. (1) All believers have some gift (*charisma*, a gift-in-grace, designed to equip Christians to contribute to the well-being of the entire community in some specific way). The worth of the individual is highlighted in vv 7-11 with emphasis on "to each person." (2) Not all have the same gift, which is clear as we mark the repetition of "different kinds" (in vv 4-6, NIV). (3) All gifts are designated to enrich the total family of believers (v 7b) and all are granted at the sovereign disposing of the Spirit (v 11, which is one side of the coin, marked by the call in 12:31; 14:1, "desire the greater spiritual gifts"—cf. 14:12—which looks to be a quote from the Corinthians themselves).

The list of nine gifts in vv 4-10 is significant; it is evidently related to the Corinthian scene, and should be treated as open-ended. Paul is giving pertinent examples, to be compared with Rom 12:6-8; 1 Thess 5:19-22; Eph 4:11 and 1 Pet 4:10, 11. The simplest way of classifying these ministries in the church is under the rubrics of teaching, accrediting, and communicating. If this is done, the need of wise teachers and scholars, authentic prophets and leaders, and effective communicators and evangelists in the church and the world is as vital today as ever. Nor should we overlook the work of those gifted with the healing art (12:28) and the expertise of administrative skills (12:28)—two gifts that happily are being rediscovered in the present time.

### (b) The Body Life

Paul's image of the church as body plays a central role, with the obvious points of connection bought out cautiously by William Baird:[3] as body the church reveals, resembles, and represents Christ. The key lies in 12:13 with its emphasis on *unity* in the midst of diversity and *multiplicity* in spite of organic unity.

The two phrases Paul employs to explain what that unity-in-diversity means are "baptism in the Spirit" (parallels with Luke 3:16; John 1:33; Acts 1:5; 11:16 show that the phrase has to do primarily with initiation into the body life) and "drinking the Spirit" (12:31, NIV; but the verb could mean "to be immersed"). Both ways of writing are rooted in experience and are "evocative," i.e., relating to calling (*vocatio*). They add up to one conclusion: the Spirit inaugurates new life and incorporates Christians into one body.

The life of that body is then outlined in 12:12-27, with four points registered: all Christians are necessary members of the body, and cannot ordinarily survive in isolation (vv 15, 16); all Christians need one another (vv 17-22); all Christians enrich one another (vv 23-25); and all Christians are involved with one another (vv 25, 26). The chief point, intended to be heeded, is v 25: "no division in the body," harking back to 1:10; 11:18, though there are special ministries within the one body (12:28-30).

### (c) The Model That Motivates

Verse 31 poses a statement as a question, "But you are eagerly desiring the greater gifts, are you?" (combining NIV and marg.). If this remark reflects the attitude of the Corinthian readers, what follows will be Paul's corrective comment in answer to the implied question: "Well, I intend to show you a still better way." At this point Paul proceeds to unpack what the "still better way" is all about: It is the way of love (*agape*, whose definition is still elusive but probably is best described by a caring attitude to those in need and a bid to identify ourselves with God's interests in other people). The point to grasp in context is that Paul is not offering love as another spiritual gift in a series; rather, he is insisting that love is the essential accompaniment of all *charismata*. Indeed, no *charisma* has effective and lasting value unless it is exercised under the control and motivation of love.

Chapter 13 was originally composed as a hymnic or lyrical piece in praise of love, just as both Jewish sages and Greek religious poets praised some aspect of God or the gods in a fulsome way. Whatever its original purpose, the lyric of love is placed here in the letter for an eminently practical reason. To the readers who were seeking (what they termed) the greater or greatest gifts of the Spirit (see 1 Cor 14:12), Paul gives the reminder that love is preeminent over all the *charismata* which cry out for *agape* to give them direction and intent (13:1–3). Moving eloquence and ecstatic speech—two notable qualities much prized at Corinth where Apollos's influence (Acts 18:24) and glossolalic utterances stood high on the approved list—need love to inform them.

The gift of intellectual prowess was also highly regarded, but Paul has already set up a danger signal (1 Cor 8:1). A practical, working faith is a desirable quality (see Mark 11:23), for by faith in God's wonderworking power great things are attempted and achieved. Yet the danger is exhibitionism and showmanship by which "faith" is paraded and made a ground of boasting. The warning given in Matt 7:22, 23 is always to be heeded. Philanthropists who give their money or even their lives (RSV marg.) to relieve the distress of the needy are a rebuke to all professed believers. But the vital issue is always one of motive (hence RSV marg. again). Accepting the translation of v 3 in RSV, NIV and most editors and commentators with the notable exception of Fee,[4] we may find here a

*The Gospel, the Spirit, and the Congregation*

climax in Paul's list: "if I hand over my body to be burned [like the martyrs of Dan 3:28], but have not love, I am not benefited at all." Again, the sacrifice of the martyr is breath-catching, but we need to recall that this is not a uniquely Jewish or Christian trait, as Buddhist monks who died in the petrol fires in Saigon, Vietnam, illustrate. Motive is once more the chief consideration, while underlining yet again Paul's insistence that all true faith works by love (Gal 5:6).

What is love anyway? The section in vv 4–7 will help us get a handle on a slippery word, often filled with all kinds of sentimental, erotic, and selfish notions. Paul's measured words that follow are helpful in recoining the much abused term. There is a statement of what love does: It is patient and kind (natural partners, as in Gal 5:22; Col 3:12; 2 Cor 6:6); there is a denial of a way of life that love abhors (no less than eight undesirable qualities, all verbs, are listed). Love is not jealous, conceited as a windbag (Arndt-Gingrich-Danker's *Lexicon*), proud (a damning sin at Corinth: see 1 Cor 4:6, 18, 19; 5:2; 8:1), rude, selfish, irritated, with an unforgiving spirit, and evilly intentioned; there is a reminder that love is not a fair-weather quality. It endures in all circumstances, especially when tested and tempted to give up:

> Love is not love
> which alters when it alteration finds.

In a final stanza Paul stresses the permanence of love (vv 8–13). The gifts of prophecy, tongues, and knowledge are all related to—because relevant for—this age. They have a value and need to be cultivated, within the constraints love also imposes (hence 14:1, 20). But their usefulness is condi-tioned by their need, whereas love, because it is an expres-sion of God's own nature (1 John 4:7–12) will last forever.

So love is supreme; it is an eschatological quality, i.e., in bringing the life of the new age into human experience, while still pointing forward to the "not-yet" element, along with faith and hope. Even so, it outshines them because (i) it is the very soul of the other gifts (vv 1–3); (ii) it is supreme by its own excellence and virtue; and (iii) it is of the essence of deity (1 John 4:16) and is seen most tellingly in him who is God incarnate (2 Cor 10:1). The last point is worth a separate mention. It is true that 1 Cor 13 does not mention specifically the name of Jesus, yet his spirit pervades it and it is his character we can see on display. For that reason, a recent expositor is led to conclude that this chapter stands out as the center of Paul's theology, and as an exquisite blend of christology, soteriology, and ethics. Her judgment[5] is accurate, and paves the way for our next chapter on the Christian life according to these Corinthian letters.

# 6    CHRISTIAN LIVING AND GIVING

The two epistles to Corinth are a wonderfully descriptive case history of an early Christian community. The church (as we saw) was made up of a motley collection of men and women recently won over from a pagan background, yet oppressed by the claims of an ever-present society whose value system still held attraction for them. So great was the pull that some believers, misinterpreting Paul's earlier letter (1 Cor 5:9, 10), wanted to quit the world altogether and form a company of recluses. Paul cannot sanction that solution to moral dilemmas. Instead, he bids them look at the issues squarely, and find a Christian vocation in the place where they live, while using every opportunity to live in harmony with one's family, if at all possible (1 Cor 7:12–16), and in freedom, if one can gain it (1 Cor 7:21). Otherwise, the directive rings out:

> As the Lord has apportioned to each person, as the Lord has called each person, so let his way of life be. (7:17)

Each person should remain in the situation which he was in when God called him [or her]. (7:20)

Each person, as responsible to God, should remain in the situation to which God called him [or her]. (7:24)

This simple-sounding counsel needed to be applied; and it can only be understood against a larger background. The Christians being addressed may be described in the following ways. Here is a résumé, which sums up our earlier discussion and brings together the coverage of both epistles.

(i) The preconversion lifestyle set down in 1 Cor 6:9-11 contains one of the fullest descriptions of the moral world from which Paul's converts came. There is a list of ten vices that marked out their "old life." The two most hotly debated terms are given as *malakoi* and *arsenokoitai*, referring to passive and active partners in homosexual activity (so NIV "male prostitutes," "homosexual offenders"; but not NEB, TEV). Other vv to be included are 1 Cor 12:2; 2 Cor 12:20, 21.

(ii) The turning point came in their response to Paul's proclamation of Christ's death and resurrection leading to new life in the Spirit (2 Cor 3:6) and a share in the new creation (2 Cor 5:17). Paul's gospel of reconciliation (2 Cor 5:18-21) had its call in a summons of "dying to live" (2 Cor 5:14, 15), certified in an acceptance of Jesus as Lord (1 Cor 12:3) and in baptism (1 Cor 6:11; 12:13) with which is linked the sealing of the Spirit (2 Cor 1:21, 22; 5:5) and the hope of resurrection which, in turn, threw moral responsibility into prominence (2 Cor 5:6-10). The practical outworking is seen in 1 Cor 15:34.

(iii) But the Corinthians were faced with a persistent danger to relapse into former ways (1 Cor 15:33; 2 Cor 6:1; 6:14-7:1), urged on by erroneous teaching that encouraged moral laxity (1 Cor 6:12; 10:23) and a false reliance on sacramental efficacy (1 Cor 1:13-15; 10:1-13). At issue—as we observed—

was the definition of what it meant to be "spiritual" (*pneumatikos*), a status claimed by certain folk in the church (1 Cor 2:13; 14:37) and leading to a debating point whether the term "spirituality" was unconnected with morality.

## Paul's exposition of the Christian life

Opposed to the enthusiasm and elitism (1 Cor 4:8; 11:19) that were rampant in a Christian fellowship that was *both* socially stratified between the rich, middle-income, poor, and slave classes *and* theologically confused and racked by dissension, Paul sets certain basic theological and ethical considerations. These are now to be listed, and in review they will sum up much of the preceding discussion.

(i) What modern scholarship has dubbed the "eschatological reservation" or "proviso" designates the way the Christian life for Paul has a built-in tension between what is now and what belongs to the future. It is the "tasiological" (from *tasis*, a Greek word for strain, tension) factor that accounts for the way in which the Christian is a person suspended between the "now" of an inaugurated salvation (1 Cor 1:18, 30; 2 Cor 6:1, 2) wrought by God's reconciling deed (2 Cor 5:19) and the "then" of a future that is promised but not yet actualized (1 Cor 15:23-28; 2 Cor 5:1-10). The church's life is set at the intersection of the two epochs (1 Cor 10:11; 13:12), straddling the past redemption and the beginning of new life-in-the-Spirit who is the "down payment" and the future consummation. The kingdom of Christ is present; the kingdom of God is future, although its signs and powers are visible now (1 Cor 6:9).

(ii) The Christian is called to live now "as if" the final salvation were a reality (1 Cor 7:29-31), with a loose attachment to the affairs of this world in anticipation of the ultimate epoch to come. The imagery of 1 Cor 5:6-8 joins together these two facets: you are unleavened bread; now clear out the leaven of moral evil by becoming what you already are (i.e., sanctified in Christ, according to 1 Cor 1:2, 30). With another image Paul states the same paradox in 2 Cor 5:1-10. We (already) *have* a building from heaven as our final destiny, but we shall not take possession of it until the earthly tent we live in is taken down in death. Only then will what is mortal be swallowed up by (eternal) life (5:4).

(iii) The sacraments are oriented to the same future, pointing forward to the Parousia (1 Cor 11:26; 16:22). If there is a false reliance on the power of religious ordinances to act irrespective of moral considerations, they contain the force of judgment (1 Cor 10:5-13; 11:27-31). When they are rightly perceived as eschatological signs connecting the "already" to the "not yet," the water of baptism and the bread-cup symbolism of the Lord's table become the focal point of unity (1 Cor 1:13; 12:13) and the means of confessing a common life that runs through the body of Christ (1 Cor 10:16, 17).

"Body" plays a significant part in Paul's understanding of the Christian life, just as *koinonia* ethics is well illustrated in 1 Cor 11:29 by the use of "body" language to apply equally to the reality behind the bread and to the corporate aspect of believers-in-fellowship at the supper meal. We turn to 1 Cor 6:12-20 to see the full range of Paul's "body" theology on display. No fewer than four meanings of "body" (*soma*) are to be seen in one short paragraph.

"Body" is normally, in our parlance, a person's physical frame, but occasionally it takes on a more inclusive sense. For instance, "everybody" really means everyone, every single person viewed as a group. Or, "When a body meets a body, coming through the rye" is Robert Burns's way of poetically describing two people meeting together. So we are preparing to consider a more complex way of regarding the body idea, found in Paul. J. Weiss[1] has put it memorably: "The body . . . [for Paul] is not only the material body

. . . but the imperishable form of the personality." It stands for the real self, the whole person, as expressed in one's physical presence in this life but pointing forward to a new existence beyond death (1 Cor 15:44-49). The specific sense Paul gives explains the puzzling verse in 1 Cor 6:18 ("he who sins sexually sins against his own body"). Union with a prostitute is an offense against the whole person—indeed against two persons, the man and the woman (6:15), and so the practice is a betrayal of Christian profession as well as a degradation of womanhood.

The section of 1 Cor 6:12-20 brings together several strands of Pauline applied theology: (a) The body has been redeemed, with a price paid for its purchase (6:20). Christians are therefore in a very real sense not their own, nor are they to please themselves. Their whole being exists for God's glory whose image they reflect (1 Cor 11:7) and whose destiny is to please him (2 Cor 5:9).

(b) The body is made holy by the Holy Spirit who indwells believers as the Presence of God filled the Jerusalem temple (1 Kgs 8:11); it is therefore to be treated with respect and dignity, never defiled or abused, since it—like the church (1 Cor 3:16, 17)—is the Spirit's shrine (6:9).

(c) The body is a member of Christ (6:15); that is, it forms part of his body, the church of which he is the head. Sexual irregularities cause damage to the integrity of the persons involved, and so deform the body of Christ by perverting the nuptial union between Christ and his bride (6:16; 2 Cor 11:2, 3).

(d) The body will be raised (6:14), which means that God has an eternal purpose for the body, albeit a "spiritual body" (1 Cor 15:44; 2 Cor 5:2, "a heavenly dwelling"), but with some connection with the human life we have known in this world. We shall give account *then* of what we have done "in the body" *now* (2 Cor 5:10). Paul cannot escape the moral claims of the theology he espoused.

(iv) The cross of Jesus also stood at the center of Paul's message and ministry at Corinth. The cross functioned—to use a current expression—in a polyvalent fashion; that is, it served to convey meaning at several levels of perception and experience. Primarily, the cross was seen by the apostle as the unique vehicle of saving grace (1 Cor 1:17, 18), announcing the reconciliation between God and the world of sinners (2 Cor 5:18–21). Yet equally it represents the paradigm of all Christian living (2 Cor 13:4) to be replicated in the experience of believers whose life is always seen by Paul as standing "under the cross" (*sub specie crucis*). As well as being the basis for salvation-in-experience (compare 2 Cor 8:9 with 2 Cor 6:9, 10), the cross sets the pattern for how Christians are to live when they are living "no longer for themselves but for him who died for them and was raised" (2 Cor 5:15). A few illustrations drawn from these two letters may usefully conclude our study:

(a) The believer is both the recipient of divine grace (2 Cor 6:1) and the person who is called to live under Christ's Lordship (2 Cor 4:5) compelled by his love (2 Cor 5:14). The teaching on reconciliation, which is central to the second letter, has this existential element much to the fore. That is, the Corinthians are appealed to as already reconciled persons (since God's deed is final and complete) who at the same time need to keep open channels along which God's grace may continue to flow. Their disaffection with the apostle has set up a blockage which Paul is concerned to remove. Hence the call is given in 2 Cor 5:20, "Be reconciled to God." God's purpose is for his people to reflect the divine image seen in Christ (1 Cor 11:3–10); at the same time they must be open to the activity of the Spirit who seeks to fashion that image in increasing clarity in their lives (2 Cor 3:18; 8:23). But this hinges on the freedom by which they are called to live; and the Lordship of Christ is the sole guarantee of that freedom (2 Cor 3:15–17; see 1 Cor 6:17: "he who unites himself to the Lord is one with him in spirit," NIV).

(b) Christians are both forgiven individuals (since as individuals they are one with the world that is already reconciled to God and they are among those whose sins are not counted against them, 2 Cor 5:19) and those who are called to show forgiveness to others who may have wronged them.

Much of 2 Cor 2:5-11 and 7:5-13 is erected on the single base of what is expected of a leader like Paul and of a congregation such as the Corinthians when faced with the moral challenge of church discipline and pardon, held in mutual tension. Paul has been affronted, but now he seeks restoration and rehabilitation for the wrongdoer. The Corinthians have been lax, then over-rigorous in punishing him; and now they are appealed to that they may act in a positive way. The oscillation of corporate behavior reaching from pride and permissiveness (1 Cor 5:1-13) through open indulgence and consent which required the "tearful letter" (2 Cor 2:4), and now to a fierce vindictiveness in meting out punishment (2 Cor 2:6), and on to a welcoming attitude to those missionaries who denigrated Paul's authority (2 Cor 11:4, 19, 20)—these are the varying moods that showed themselves among the apostle's readers.

(c) Paul's authority as the pioneer apostle and church builder (1 Cor 3:5-10; 2 Cor 10:13-18) is one that in turn is to be understood and evaluated according to the paradox that runs through both epistles. One example comes in 1 Cor 4:9-21 with its twin notes of Paul's frailty and social disgrace, on the one side, and his strong attitudes which wield the rod of discipline and punishment, on the other (v 21, KJV/AV). Another example can be seen in 2 Cor 6:3-10 with its "litany of woes" to offset his status as one of the "servants of God" charged to fulfill a ministry that God gave him to exercise authority (2 Cor 13:10; cf. 10:8-11). The key to this strange amalgam of ideas is to be found in what happened to the Lord himself: He was rich and became poor for our sake (2 Cor 8:9); he was Lord but was crucified in weakness (2 Cor 13:4a), yet he is still Lord. And we are like him, concludes Paul (13:4b)—weak yet strong, with a strength held in restraint and exercised always in love (2 Cor 5:14) and as servants, not lords, of the people of God (2 Cor 1:24).

(d) Finally, as a result of the good effect of the "severe letter" (2 Cor 7:8) and the clearing of the air at Corinth with the storm clouds of rebellion lifted, Paul believed, it was time to reintroduce the topic of the collection for the saints (1 Cor 16:1–4). Titus was instructed to set the process in motion (2 Cor 8:6, 16, 17) since he had brought the good report on the Corinthians' change of heart to Paul (2 Cor 7:13–16).

The church of Corinth, already known to be endowed with many graces (1 Cor 1:7), is therefore encouraged to "overflow in this gracious service as well." The "grace" (charis) referred to is responsiveness to human need, represented by the poor saints of the Jerusalem church, and the sign that the Gentiles were one with the mother church in the capital city of the ancestral faith. There is also an eschatological side to Paul's plan to raise the collection; he explains this in Rom 15:19–33 which announces that Paul has wound up his missionary service in the east (from Jerusalem to Illyricum [Yugoslavia] forming a northeast quadrant in the ancient world) and is on his way to Rome and beyond. In that way, with his mission work completed, there is the prospect of a "full number of the Gentiles" brought in to the church as a prelude to the end time when the Deliverer will come from Zion (Rom 11:25, 26). The sign of that final consummation of the ages is that the Gentiles will make a pilgrimage to the holy city, as the prophets foretold (Isa 2:1–5; Mic 4:1–5). He sees his visit to Jerusalem with the Gentiles' offerings and with Gentile delegates in attendance (2 Cor 8:18–24; 9:5) as the final piece in the jig-saw puzzle that will come into place as a mark of the fulfillment of God's ancient plan.

It is clear, then, that several strands of Christian conviction and belief came together in Paul's desire to help financially the distressed church in Zion—Christian compassion for the needy (Gal 2:10), a tangible expression of unity to cement relations between the two ethnic wings of the one church, and the furthering of divine purposes leading to the wind-up of the ages. These are all part of Paul's motivation.

Yet the most obvious reason for the collection should not be passed over. Paul is seeking to extract from the Corinthians a fulfillment of their earlier pledge to assist him. In such a way they will be giving proof of the sincerity and reality of their loyalty to him and his apostolic authority.

Some pieces of evidence support this conclusion (2 Cor 8:8): (i) in all this discussion through chs 8 and 9 he never once mentions "money" as such; instead his terms are either borrowed from the liturgical idioms of the Old Testament ("offering," "service" [*leitourgia*]) or speak of the spirit that should lead people to give ("fellowship" [*koinonia*], "blessing"). (ii) His appeal to the generosity of the Macedonians (2 Cor 8:1-7; 9:2, 13) underlines the way those congregations, such as Philippi (Phil 1:5; 4:10-19), were consistently true in their affection for him and practical in their support of his apostolic ministry. (iii) The example of men like Titus and other unnamed leaders (2 Cor 8:18-24; 9:3) shows how highly Paul regarded them as faithful friends and coworkers. Colleagueship is one trait Paul valued; but more than that, "they are the glory of Christ" (8:23, lit. transl.) which surely goes back to 2 Cor 3:18. The Spirit's work is to transform believers into Christ's image; these men are living embodiments of that design—and they are Paul's supporters.

(iv) And, in 2 Cor 9:7, 8 Paul lifts up the true spirit of giving as an exercise that shows how well his entire gospel has been understood:

Let each one give as he has decided in his mind, not regretfully nor under constraint: for it is the cheerful giver that God loves. God is able to make all grace to overflow to you, so that, in all things and at all times, you may have all you need and may overflow in every kind of good work.

The Corinthians who read these pungent words would recall the whole debate over "spiritual gifts" which had been ventilated in their assembly. Now Paul says the last word on the topic. It is an encouragement to give to others as freely as we have received from God, not treating our giftedness as a selfish possession (as 1 Cor 4:7; 13:1-3) but seeing it as a way to build up the body of Christ, whether at Corinth or in Jerusalem. It is a reminder that we share in Christ a common life whose hallmark is a true spirit of *koinonia* with him and our fellow Christians (1 Cor 10:16, 17; 12:7, 11, 12). And it is a call to gratitude that answers God's gift of grace. Writes the apostle with a deliberate play on the word *charis*:

You are lacking in no *charisma*, his gift-in-grace. (1 Cor 1:7)

You know the grace (*charis*) of the Lord Jesus Christ. (2 Cor 8:9; 13:14)

You have received God's grace (*charis*) in great measure. (2 Cor 9:8)

You are responding to the grace (*charis*) of Paul's apostleship. (1 Cor 15:10)

Now, thanks (*charis*) be to God for his gift beyond measure! (2 Cor 9:15)

*Christian Living and Giving*

# NOTES

### Preface

1. William Baird, *The Corinthian Church–A Biblical Approach to Urban Culture* (New York: Abingdon, 1964); E. A. Judge, *The Social Patterns of Christian Groups in the First Century* (London: Tyndale Press, 1960); W. A. Meeks, *The First Urban Christians. The Social World of the Apostle Paul* (New Haven: Yale University Press, 1983); Gerd Theissen, *The Social Setting of Pauline Christianity: Essays on Corinth* (Philadelphia: Fortress Press, 1982).

2. J. Murphy-O'Connor, *St Paul's Corinth: Texts and Archaeology* (Wilmington, Del.: M. Glazier, Inc., 1983); P. Marshall, *Enmity in Corinth* (Tübingen: Mohr, 1987); C. H. Talbert, *Reading Corinthians. A Literary and Theological Commentary on 1 and 2 Corinthians* (New York: Crossroad, 1987).

3. C. K. Barrett, *A Commentary on the Second Epistle to the Corinthians* (New York: Harper and Row, 1973), 322.

### Chapter 1    Paul's Friends at Corinth

1. A. Deissmann, *Light from the Ancient East* (London: Hodder and Stoughton, 1927), 144.

2. E. A. Judge, *Social Patterns*, 58.

3. G. Theissen, *Social Setting*, 69–73.

4. See V. P. Furnish, "Corinth in Paul's Time," *Biblical Archaeological Review* 15, 1988, 15–27.

5. N. A. Dahl, *Studies in Paul* (Minneapolis: Augsburg, 1977), 40–61.

**Chapter 2  Paul's Apostolic Service in Theory and Practice**
1. C. K. Barrett, *A Commentary on the First Epistle to the Corinthians* (New York: Harper and Row, 1968), ad loc.

**Chapter 3  The God and Father of Our Lord Jesus Christ**
1. H. Conzelmann, *1 Corinthians* (Philadelphia: Fortress Press, 1975), Introduction.
2. W. M. Ramsay, *The Cities of St. Paul* (New York: Longmans, 1908).
3. E. Käsemann, *Essays on New Testament Themes* (Naperville, Ill.: Allenson, 1964), ch 3, discussed in R. P. Martin, *The Spirit and the Congregation* (Grand Rapids: Eerdmans, 1984), ch 1.
4. J. Hainz, *Koinonia. Kirche als Gemeinschaft bei Paulus* (Regensburg: Pustet, 1972), 61.

**Chapter 4  The Grace and Glory of Our Lord Jesus Christ**
1. G. D. Fee, *The First Epistle to the Corinthians* (Grand Rapids: Eerdmans, 1987), 448–49.
2. V. P. Furnish, "Corinth in Paul's Time," 25, 26.

**Chapter 5  The Gospel, the Spirit, and the Congregation**
1. C. K. Barrett, *Essays on Paul* (Philadelphia: Westminster Press, 1982), 6–14.
2. J. Moffatt, *The First Epistle of Paul to the Corinthians* (London: Hodder and Stoughton, 1938), ad loc.
3. W. Baird, *1 Corinthians, 2 Corinthians* (Atlanta: John Knox, 1980), 52.
4. Fee, *First Corinthians*, 634.
5. O. Wischmeyer, *Der höchste Weg. Das 13. Kapitel des Korintherbriefes* (Gütersloh: Gütersloher Verlag, 1981), 230–33.

**Chapter 6  Christian Living and Giving**
1. J. Weiss, *Der erste Korintherbrief* (Göttingen: Vandenhoeck und Ruprecht, 1910), ad loc.

# INDEX OF SCRIPTURES

**ABBREVIATIONS**

AV/KJV   Authorized Version/King James Version

*Leg. All.*   The Allegory of the Laws (Philo)

LXX   Septuagint, Greek translation of the Old Testament

NEB   New English Bible

NIV   New International Version

RSV   Revised Standard Version

TEV   Today's English Version

*Index of Scriptures*